WHAT GREAT TEAMS DO GREAT

David Wheatley, John Barrett and **Christi Barrett** work together at Humanergy, a leadership development company with the mission to create a new kind of leader committed to the greater good and with the character, wisdom and competence to make a real difference in their teams, organizations and even the world. Over the past twenty-five years, the authors have worked with about 375 different organizations, training and coaching their leaders and teams and facilitating key transitions. John Barrett and David Wheatley previously authored *50 DOs for Everyday Leadership*. Christi Barrett is the co-author of *In Whose Best Interest: One Child's Odyssey, A Nation's Responsibility* and *Putting Connectedness, Continuity, Dignity and Opportunity to Work*.

Praise for

WHAT GREAT TEAMS DO GREAT

"The authors dispel the myth that great teams just happen organically; they take work at the individual, collective, and leadership levels. Leaders and managers must be thoughtful and deliberate about how to ensure everyone takes personal (and collective) responsibility for the team's performance. The framework presented in Chapter 1 is such a useful guide that serves as an important gut check to all who engage in teams and support teams. I will be using this framework in my own work and as I work with others in my role as a higher education educator and consultant."

—Vicki L. Baker, MBA, MS, PhD
Professor, Economics and Management, Albion College; Co-Founder, Lead Mentor Develop

"*What Great Teams Do Great* is an extremely useful collection of concepts that dissect the workings of a team and provide the tools to form great ones. Putting these tools and visuals into practice and following the Green Path truly produces extraordinary organizational results and multiplies the individual contribution many times over."

—Brian Lundquist
Chief Global Supply Officer, Sundial Growers

"Applying GREAT ideas and information from this GREAT book into life and work will make ordinary people become GREAT."

—Colonel Nguyet Tran
Viet Nam Ministry of Public Security

"I didn't realize why my day-to-day felt so monotonous until I read about the habit loop, and how to break that habit. I feel energized and ready to break that habit and look at my job in a new way. I enjoyed *What Great Teams Do Great* very much and look forward to applying it in our company setting."

—Marlo Palermo
Shift Supervisor, Brazeway, Inc.

"I have spent thirty years working with teams, leadership and corporate cultures. For the most part, it's not hard to build great teams, become great leaders and sustain corporate cultures that support the purpose of the team. It's usually an issue of personal ego or lack of understanding that prevents us from reaching our goal.
"In their book *What Great Teams Do Great*, David Wheatley, John Barrett and Christi Barrett lay out the simple principles of being great. They are simple to state but difficult to execute (see above). However, by stating the principles so directly and succinctly, this book provides the guidelines to accomplish that goal.
"Follow the guidelines and perspectives they set. You'll be greatly rewarded with lasting success."

—Ron Potter
Founding Partner, Team Leadership Culture

"Never has there been a more timely publication. Businesses and nonprofits are going to be severely challenged to come up with strategies to survive in this new world we find ourselves in. Learning how to form and run successful groups in our organizations will be invaluable."

—Mary Jo Byrne
Executive Director, Fountain Clinic

"This book is an easy-to-read guide accessible not only to organizational leaders, but to members of any workplace team who want to increase their understanding of how great teams function. Bolstered by extensive experience in the field, solid research, and real-world examples, *What Great Teams Do Great* illustrates how all team members can commit to better choices, change bad habits to good ones, take the 'green path' of good communication and transform their teams. The tools offered, along with the emphasis on the need to make 'green path choices' helped our staff community at the Fetzer Institute towards developing positive and constructive work culture. The experience the authors bring to this endeavor is invaluable to anyone, from upper management to entry-level, who wants to contribute to greater teamwork in their organization."

—Bob Boisture
President and Chief Executive Officer, Fetzer Institute

"The best performing teams are committed to both a culture of introspection as well as the drive to do the right thing day in and day out. *What Great Teams Do Great* identifies the drivers, and more importantly the motivators, to success. Seasoned leaders, aspiring future leaders and team members will all benefit from *What Great Teams Do Great*."

—Joel Wittenberg
Vice President and Chief Investment Officer, WK Kellogg Foundation

"The *What Great Teams Do Great* model is a tool that teams and leaders in today's world need to embrace and understand in order to fully recognize their full collective potential."

—Ken E. Biddle
General Manager, Aerospace Industry

"David, John and Christi have a unique ability to transform a complex concept into an intuitive visual representation and show that it really is all common sense. Leadership via a Green Path is something I strive to do each and every day."

—Mike Kohout
Chief Operating Officer, Vantage Elevation

"*What Great Teams Do Great* is a must read for all leaders, front line to executives. Using David, John, and Christi's main drivers of care, commitment, and people to inform transformative choices will help lead your team down a path of greatness."

—Robb Smalldon
President, Landscape Forms

"*What Great Teams Do Great* is an exemplary concise book that presents practical, easy-to-understand and well-structured tools and models to understand and improve team performance based on years of experience—and which have proven to deliver great results in my own organization!"

—Magnus Gäfvert
Chief Executive Officer, Modelon

"The Humanergy team has a unique talent to hit home with lasting points that revolutionize team actions, decision-making, and pace. *What Great Teams Do Great* drives home critical behavioral tools that have transformed our business process and team culture."

—Stephanie Hickman Boyse
Retired Chief Executive Officer and Director, Brazeway, Inc.

"A key book for not only business leadership, but to lead through life in a true and connected human way in a time when assumptions cloud good leadership decision-making. This is one of those books that will have a tattered cover and notes in the margins because it is a tool that will be used by leaders and aspiring leaders as they work with each other and their teams."

—Scott McFarland
Chief Executive Officer, Honor Credit Union

"In the theme of teamwork, human nature is the most powerful and constant factor in business and certainly in life. The tools and practices outlined in this book are a great means to not just survive but to succeed in the world of teams. Whether they are business, academic, community or other forms of teamwork, utilizing these principles will benefit you and your enterprise."

—Daniel E. Sceli
Chief Executive Officer, Cadillac Products Automotive Company

"While a lot has been written on teamwork, I can't remember the last time I picked up a book and had so many 'Aha' moments. Filled with simple, straightforward, practical steps anyone can do to improve their work within a team, this book spoke to me at a level where I actually exist on a daily basis. Instead of looking at 'teamwork' or 'leadership' as mysterious, ethereal or hard-to-attain concepts, it puts forward an easy-to-understand framework for actually making better decisions. If you read this book once, you will be inspired. If you use it on a regular basis, you will be transformed."

—Mary R. Flack, MD
Executive Director, Inflammation, Boehringer-Ingelheim Pharma

"*What Great Teams Do Great* presents a fresh and compelling lens to understand and activate the ways in which I can be a much better team leader and participant. David, John, and Christi offer a simple model of choices and processes which can unravel and improve what can become seemingly complicated team dynamics into a clear direction along the green path!"

—Michael A. Roeder
President and Chief Operating Officer, Fabri-Kal Corporation

"*What Great Teams Do Great* is a useful guide for your team, regardless of your company's size or industry you work in. Practical, straightforward and easy to apply."

—Liz Winninger
President and Chief Executive Officer, Xtend Credit Union

"In our fast-paced, technology-driven world, building a high-performing team is more critical than ever. *What Great Teams Do Great* will show you the proven steps to transform and move your team to the next level and beyond. Leaders who read this book and apply the techniques will see immediate results on all business fronts."

—John F. Clark
President and Chief Executive Officer, National Center for Missing and Exploited Children

"*What Great Teams Do Great* unravels how teams operate and gives you the key tools to set your team on the path to success! I highly recommend *What Great Teams Do Great* for anyone who wishes to understand the working of a team, and leverage its key concepts to bring your team to the next level."

—Pieter Dermont
Director, Business Development, Modelon

"Books focusing on leadership are plentiful. The world is full of leadership coaches. Practically speaking, though, everyone has the potential to make leadership choices that influence the success of a team, and the authors of *What Great Teams Do Great* recognize this reality. By providing a roadmap that breaks down leadership choices for the individual, *What Great Teams Do Great* establishes a framework that shifts the power over the success of the team to individual team members themselves."

—Sean P. Fahey
Senior Federal Law Enforcement Officer

"A must read for anyone who is part of a team. Regardless of tenure or title, this book gives practical leadership and collaboration tips you can implement immediately. . . . We've implemented many of the high-performing teams methods at our company. This book is a condensed version of what took us years to implement. Should be required reading for professionals."

—Conor Macfarlane
President and Chief Executive Officer, 3Eye Technologies

"Unfortunately, many of us have been on dysfunctional teams at one point or another. This book is a good summary of why this happens and what organizations can do to plan for more efficient execution. It explores the human dynamics behind high-performance teams and outlines simple steps to create the opportunity to launch and maintain highly effective teams. A fast read that should be required for existing and new teams."

Daniel Di Sebastian, President and Chief Executive Officer, Fontana America Inc. at FONTANA GRUPPO

WHAT GREAT TEAMS DO GREAT

How Ordinary People Accomplish the Extraordinary

DAVID WHEATLEY, JOHN BARRETT AND CHRISTI BARRETT

Published by
Rupa Publications India Pvt. Ltd 2025
7/16, Ansari Road, Daryaganj
New Delhi 110002

Sales centres:
Bengaluru Chennai
Hyderabad Jaipur Kathmandu
Kolkata Mumbai Prayagraj

Copyright © David Wheatley, John Barrett and Christi Barrett 2025
Original English language edition published by Koehler Books 3705 Shore
Arranged via Licensor's Agent: DropCap Inc.
Drive, Virginia Beach Virginia 23455, USA

The views and opinions expressed in this book are the authors'
own and the facts are as reported by them which have been
verified to the extent possible, and the publishers are not in
any way liable for the same.

All rights reserved.
No part of this publication may be reproduced, transmitted,
or stored in a retrieval system, in any form or by any means, electronic,
mechanical, photocopying, recording or otherwise, without the prior
permission of the publisher.

P-ISBN: 978-93-5702-885-1
E-ISBN: 978-93-5702-920-9

First impression 2025

10 9 8 7 6 5 4 3 2 1

The moral right of the authors has been asserted.

Printed in India

This book is sold subject to the condition that it shall not, by way of
trade or otherwise, be lent, resold, hired out, or otherwise circulated,
without the publisher's prior consent, in any form of binding or
cover other than that in which it is published.

TABLE OF CONTENTS

Introduction 1

Chapter 1: Teams... 4
Chapter 2: Leadership, Teamwork and Choice 8
Chapter 3: Changing Choices 22
Chapter 4: Choices and Processes 35
Chapter 5: Navigating Issues 56
Chapter 6: Making Your Team Great........................ 63
Chapter 7: What Great Teams Do Great in Action........... 68
Chapter 8: Issues and Answers 80

Appendices 89
Glossary... 91
Acknowledgments.. 97

INTRODUCTION

THINK OF A GREAT team—one that was a joy to be part of, or perhaps one that you observed and aspired to join. Consider exemplary groups of people you've heard of who worked well together and got things done. Whether it's a team you have participated in or just heard of, what made these great teams so great?

We have been working with teams collectively for over seventy-five years. Rather than "talking at" people about the ins and outs of great teams, we always love to start by engaging them.

When we asked groups of people to talk about teamwork in general, we typically got textbook answers. So instead, we asked them to reflect on a great team they had experienced. At least 90 percent had been a part of a great team, or at least seen one from a distance.

When asked to describe the experience, their answers had magic in their content and enthusiasm in their delivery. We heard general comments like *powerful, amazing, life-changing, impactful, energizing, super-productive, game-changing, challenging, supportive, made me eager to jump out of bed in the morning, wow,* etc.

We want everyone to have the experience of a great team. If only we could snap our fingers and create amazing teams everywhere—at work, in volunteer capacities and in education!

However, great teams don't happen by magic, even if the experience of belonging to one does seem charmed. So we continue by asking, "What does a great team DO great?"

We always received a flood of responses, because the answers were energized by the wonderful experience of great teams (and, as you will see, by the horrific involvement with lousy teams).

Here are some specific examples of the spontaneous comments we have heard from people when they reflect on the specific behaviors and results of outstanding teams.

They know what they are supposed to accomplish. They are clear and specific about the guiding principles and values that deliver results.

They are 100 percent bought into their common goals. They know their individual roles and responsibilities that contribute to team results.

They have a bias for action. They pitch in to support each other.

When things go wrong, they don't sweep it under the rug or blame individuals. They talk openly, engage creatively and create a plan to improve performance.

They communicate directly, honestly and from a basis of care. They always focus on improvement, innovation and solutions to problems.

We all recognize a great team when we see or experience one. Yet creating such first-rate team performance can feel almost impossible or at least like rocket science—complicated and even mysterious.

Why do so many people report teamwork as being one of the most difficult aspects of any work? It's because humans are involved, and people are complicated. We bring different values, personalities, cultures, beliefs, habits and experiences to the team. Plus, we naively assume that teamwork should be natural. And unfortunately, it's not. In daily practice, it's far too easy to avoid issues, give lip service to teamwork practices, or make other choices that derail the team.

Great teamwork may not be easy or simplistic, but it is attainable.

Creating a great team is possible, by combining the power of choice with some universal team processes. You can transform your existing team or build a new, great team from scratch.

The practices of *what great teams do great* lead to fewer headaches and arguments. And sometimes they even make teamwork fun.

Let's get started.

INTRODUCTION

IMPACT CYCLE — Do we have the right team? Are we truly aligned?

SET UP TEAM
- Who are we?
- What is our external reality?
- What do we need to achieve and why?
- What are our values and non-negotiable behaviors for working together?

IMPROVEMENT CYCLE — Is this the right plan?

PLAN WORK
- What are our deliverables?
- What resources do we need?
- What will we do?
- Who will do what?
- How will we communicate?

DISCIPLINE CYCLE — Are we doing what we said?

DO WORK
- Implement the plan
- Communicate / Coordinate
- Meet / Check-in
- Make decisions
- Problem solve
- Support

RESOLVE ISSUES
- Innovations / Best practices
- Opportunities
- Under performance
- Misunderstandings
- Dropped balls
- Stress
- Conflict

GREEN PATH
- Caring, honest, and direct
- Listen to understand
- Engage, align, learn, and coordinate
- Share perspectives (data driven)
- Focus forward on solutions

CHAPTER 1: TEAMS

TEAMWORK, THOUGH IT'S BANTERED about as if we all understand it the same way, is actually a rather imprecise term. The Merriam-Webster Dictionary definition of a team is "a number of persons associated together in work or activity." The definition may be simple, but it is deceptively difficult to bring complex humans together to accomplish common goals.

Teamwork is often taken for granted. We don't formally learn about teamwork best practices in school or in most work environments. So much of what we know about teamwork is based on motivational posters. (Remember the flock of birds in formation or the rowing team?) or quotations like, "There is no I in team." (By the way, there are a bunch of *I*s in every team we've ever seen.)

What is the nature of teams? Like the venerable Merriam-Webster Dictionary, we define a team as any group with a shared purpose. Teams can be transient and disband as projects are completed. Some teams exist and evolve over long periods of time. Teams can have names and mission statements and complex structures. A team can also be just two people who need to get something done together.

Regardless of the composition, longevity or formality, teams become necessary when it would be impossible to work alone and achieve the same result. And since so much of what must be done requires more than one brain, understanding teams and helping them function at their peak is of the utmost importance.

WHAT IS TEAMWORK?

Teamwork is how people accomplish their purpose(s) together. Even the most casual teams must collaborate, cooperate and coordinate their work. With varying degrees of success, teams organize and focus thinking and creativity. The glue that keeps a team together is mutual responsibility for success, and an understanding by the team's members that they couldn't be successful if they chose to go it alone.

But how do teams achieve high performance? What are the "secret sauces" that are the difference makers? What elevates teams to greatness?

The purpose of this book is to pull back the curtain to find out what great teams do great. How do they come together, stay together and achieve outstanding results?

We'll share this story of greatness without the classic inspirational narrative. (Sorry, no fish or cheese or parables or fables.) You'll also find a lack of generals, CEOs and big-name folks—the people who are typically profiled in leadership and teamwork books. With all due respect to these distinguished individuals, this book is about ordinary people accomplishing extraordinary things together. We weave in real-life examples of how people come together, get things done, enjoy the process and even surprise themselves at what they accomplish.

WONDER IF THIS BOOK REALLY APPLIES TO YOU?

"I'm not a team leader."

Whether you're a team leader or a member of the team with no formal leadership role, every person can step up to make the best of a team's potential become reality. All great teams recognize that every single person can choose to be a leader.

"My team isn't associated with a paid job."

While most teams we reference function within a company, volunteer groups can also benefit from improving team functioning. If you're thrown together with a small group to accomplish a task without pay, you too will find this book helpful in understanding the essential practices that lead to success.

"My team has been in existence for a long (or short) time."

The practical strategies in this book will help you build a new team or improve the performance of one that's ongoing. These recommended methods will include behaviors and tools you can use at any stage of your team's development, whether newly formed or with years of experience working together.

"My team is awesome already."

There certainly are great teams operating today. (Lucky you, if that is your current team experience!) The challenge is to stay great, and that takes ongoing work. Let's be clear that great doesn't mean perfect. The perfect team is a myth. And, unfortunately, if you think you've "arrived" as a group, you've begun the slow (or not-so-slow) decline into team dysfunction. It's just too easy to slip into bad practices. Gravity isn't working in any team's favor, so great teams routinely examine what's going well and what needs improvement. Even great teams must consistently work to stay great.

THE ROOTS OF THESE IDEAS

These tools and processes are based on how teams really function. While we are well-versed in research and theory, *What Great Teams Do Great* (WGTDG) grew out of team practice and how people really operate as part of a group. Specifically, WGTDG is based on our collective experiences working with teams over the past twenty-five years. We are indebted to the many people who shared their team experiences with us—the good, the bad, the ugly . . . and the great!

We share some of their stories in Chapter 7, and because we value their privacy, we have changed many of the identifying details of the teams we profile. In some cases, two or more team examples are blended together to better illustrate the best practices of What Great Teams Do Great.

CHAPTER 2: LEADERSHIP, TEAMWORK AND CHOICE

WHAT MAKES YOU A LEADER?

IN THE PAST, LEADERSHIP was associated with a particular position, title or rank within the organization. There were leaders and there were followers, and the line between those two categories was perceived to be solid. You were a leader or you were a follower.

Today, leadership is recognized to be a lot more fluid and dynamic. In the context of teamwork, it isn't just the identified team leader who exercises leadership. Every team member can act as a leader. Indeed, leadership can be exercised by individuals with no direct authority, simply by the power of a choice.

Being a successful manager or positional leader does take significant experience, mentoring, coaching and training. Yet even in formal roles, being a true leader requires more than the right title, knowledge or even skill.

Leadership requires the right mindset and skills. And leadership is more than good intentions or attitude. It is about doing. Whether you are a team leader or a team member, leadership is conveyed through the choices you make at every moment of every day.

LEADERSHIP CHOICES

Choices can be easy to spot when there is an emergency. A firefighter rushes into a burning building, in spite of the danger. A business owner responds quickly to drastic market changes that might otherwise doom the company.

Choosing to act like a leader isn't always dramatic. The majority of leadership choices are a habitual way of behaving, something that people engage in as a matter of routine. In emergencies and daily routine, people fall back on what is comfortable most of the time. That's why our daily choices don't feel like conscious decisions.

Humans are creatures of habit. We simply don't stop to consider that there may be another way of being. And yet there is. In this simple fact lies great possibility—the opportunity to tune in and choose a different behavior from the one that is on autopilot.

Take the example of a maintenance worker, Margot, who sees a peer struggling to complete a task. Margot is busy already. She can walk by, saying to herself, "Not my problem." Or Margot can stop, ask a question or offer help. Noticing a team member's dilemma and getting involved in a helpful way is a choice to act like a leader, even when it's not required.

Regardless of the role or the specific situation, being a leader means stepping up and taking ownership for who we are, what we do and what matters most. It means being aware of choice points and not just going with the flow. It means stepping away from the automatic mode from stimulus ("He insulted me") to response ("I'll show him").

A leader recognizes the choice spaces that present themselves throughout every day, and makes a conscious decision about how to respond.

Choices are powerful. As Stephen Covey said in his groundbreaking book, *The Seven Habits of Highly Effective People: Powerful Lessons in Personal Change*, "Our unique human endowments lift us above the animal world. The extent to which we exercise and develop these endowments empowers us to fulfill our uniquely human potential. Between stimulus and response is our greatest power—the freedom to choose."[1]

Examining daily choices is important to living an intentional life—one that enables a person to achieve their goals, engage in meaningful relationships and get things done with others. William Glasser, MD, a renowned psychiatrist, introduced Choice Theory in 1998.[2] One of the basic tenets is that we can only control our own choices and behaviors, not the choices or behaviors of others. Dr. Glasser believes that we are genetically programmed to satisfy four psychological needs—love and belonging, power, freedom and fun.

How do we leaders (and all humans) meet—or at least try to meet—those needs? Through choosing our own behavior.

Make no mistake. Exercising choice may be frequent and habitual, but doing so with intention is not common or easy. "Going with your gut" is a common practice and has its advantages. It's quick and familiar and comforting.

Slowing down to consciously decide how to react may seem like it's too slow and cumbersome. How will you get anything done if you have to stop and think about every situation you encounter? The answer isn't to laboriously overthink every situation. It begins with slowing down long enough to notice what is really going on, particularly when a situation is important.

Though it doesn't have to take a great deal of time, making a choice to step up is often difficult and requires discipline and real intention. This is especially true in teamwork. Our work with others can elicit a myriad of feelings that are intense, even unpleasant. And these frustrations or anxieties may appear to lead to inevitable reactions that do not feel like choices—to lash out or retreat from conflict, for example.

---

1   Covey, S., *The Seven Habits of Highly Effective People: Powerful Lessons in Personal Change.* New York: Simon and Schuster, 1989.

2   Glasser, W., *Choice Theory: A New Psychology of Personal Freedom.* 1st HarperPerennial ed. New York: HarperPerennial, 1999.

However, though people do not choose their feelings, they do choose how they react to those feelings. Nobody and no situation *makes* anyone do anything.

All team members, regardless of their actual job or role, make choices every day, whether they pause long enough to be aware of them or not. In the next section, we'll examine the nature of these choices.

TYPES OF CHOICES ≠ TYPES OF PEOPLE

As we dive into the characteristics of choices, it is important to understand that the types of choices do not mean types of people. Yes, some people seem to make a habit of choosing certain kinds of behaviors. Yet on any given day, at any moment, those same people could choose something different. They could take a different path—with a new outcome—simply by making a new type of choice.

In our work with teams, the fundamental building block of greatness (or not-so-greatness) boils down to the choices that individuals make, and thus, by extension, the choices made by the team collectively.

COMPONENTS OF CHOICES

Individual choices are built from three interdependent and fundamental motivations—CARE for the greater good (vs. just self), COMMITMENT to impact (vs. comfort) and PEOPLE understanding (vs. indifference or lack of skill in emotional calibration and interpersonal interactions).

Together, these aggregate team choices mean that the team is on one path or another—the Green Path or the Red Path. We'll share more about the paths in Chapter 4. For now, let's closely examine choices and how they impact a team.

THREE ELEMENTS OF CHOICES

A youth soccer team has finished a game. All parents are expected to stay to help take down the goal nets. Though everyone has been informed of this responsibility in advance of the game, a variety of behaviors are exhibited by the team's parents at the end of the match. In each person's choice (in fact, inherent in all choices), three elements are in play and influence the group's outcomes.

FOCUS OF CARE

The first element of choice is the focus of CARE. Are you purely driven to satisfy yourself and your own needs, or are you concerned for the greater good? Focus of care can be thought of along a continuum between a 100 percent self-focus to a 100 percent greater-good orientation.

A greater-good choice doesn't mean you sacrifice yourself completely. It simply means you're driven by something in addition to your own benefit. Inherent in this greater-good orientation is a broader focus and concern for the impact of the choice on others.

CARE for the greater good recognizes the reality of synergy—that we can do more/better together than we could ever accomplish separately. Having a greater-good focus means that you see the bigger picture and recognize that success is interconnected. What Person A can achieve affects Person B, and so on and so on.

CARE for the greater good is not just altruistic. The orientation to the best interests of all is the best way to get great results when working with others.

In our soccer parent example, each parent can focus solely on themselves and leave without giving a thought to the impact on others. Or the parent can orient to the greater good, and decide to stay and take an active or at least somewhat helpful part in putting away the nets after the game.

COMMITMENT TO IMPACT

First, what is the impact? Impact is the result of your result, or the carry-on effects of achieving the team's desired outcomes. Great teams not only orient to goals, they also want to see the difference these results will make in their corner of the world.

People making choices with a strong COMMITMENT to impact are all in. They have an enthusiasm and desire to meet and exceed objectives, and they're willing to stick with it, even in the face of obstacles and frustration. People making high-COMMITMENT-to-impact choices will think ahead, take ownership and manage time, resources and processes to ensure that goals are accomplished. Sometimes these choices aren't easy, but people making high-COMMITMENT-to-impact choices will defer comfort because they really want to make a difference.

They are tenacious and adapt as situations evolve, so that their actions contribute to success. They maintain a sense of urgency for real and meaningful results, even when faced with roadblocks or delays. High-COMMITMENT-to-impact choices focus on operating efficiently, but never sacrifice effectiveness or excellence to get something done quickly or easily.

People making choices with very low COMMITMENT to impact lack motivation and tend to give up when the going gets tough or even just uncomfortable. Those exhibiting low-COMMITMENT-to-impact choices may help others, but they avoid taking ownership for solving problems, tend to procrastinate, and allow interruptions to derail their focus. People making low-COMMITMENT choices want to remain comfortable, act out of well-established habits and not rock the boat.

High-COMMITMENT-to-impact choices can be focused on the self exclusively or include the well-being of the whole group (CARE for the greater good). What these high-COMMITMENT choices have in common is a determination and drive to achieve the outcome they want.

In the soccer example, a parent making a high-COMMITMENT-to-impact choice will actively seek to achieve what he or she wants. If they make high-COMMITMENT-to-impact choices and want to avoid doing the work, they'll do whatever it takes to make sure their needs are met and they aren't involved in taking down the goals. They may leave just as the game is finished, so the option of helping is completely eliminated. If they want what's right for the group (CARE for greater good), a parent making high-COMMITMENT-to-impact choices will ensure the nets are put away properly. If that means pitching in and encouraging/teaching others to help, that's what they will do to ensure the goal nets get stored properly.

CARE + COMMITMENT = 4 CHOICES OF LEADERSHIP

Take into account the first two elements of daily choices, and there are four different types of choices (Figure 1). (Remember that it's four different types of *choices*, not different types of *people*. Each new situation presents an opportunity to make a different type of choice, so do not label people, just the types of choices they typically make.)

People making *destructive* choices are interested only in themselves and exhibit a sustained high-intensity passion and COMMITMENT to achieving their own desires. *Passive* choices are similarly self-focused, but lack the COMMITMENT and staying power to make sure that their own ends are achieved.

Productive choices happen when people want what's best for the greater good and yet don't apply the focused intensity to ensure it happens. An obstacle, difficulty, distraction or delay can easily derail their good intentions. People making *transformative* choices are passionate about the best interests of the greater good, and they'll work diligently in the face of obstacles to make sure it happens. Transformative choices are "all-in" behaviors focused on the best results for everyone (CARE for greater good).

If our soccer parents have high CARE for the greater good combined with a strong COMMITMENT to doing the right thing, they are in the transformative choice space. They coordinate and actively engage with the other parents to make sure the nets are taken down and put away properly. Those parents may feel an urge to leave right after the game, but they choose not to act on those feelings. Instead, they focus on the team and make the transformative choice, pitch in and even make sure their collective job is done and done well.

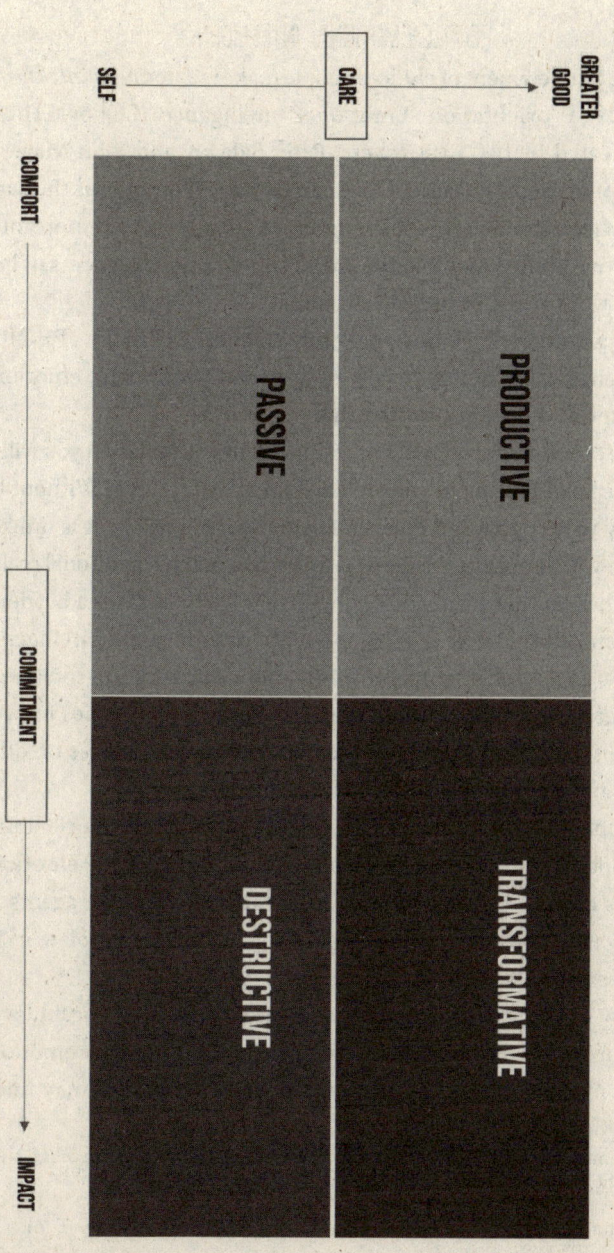

Figure 1

PEOPLE: EMOTIONAL INTELLIGENCE

The third element of choices people make is *emotional intelligence* or PEOPLE orientation. Emotional intelligence (EQ or EI) is a term created by two researchers, Peter Salavoy and John Mayer. It was popularized by Daniel Goleman in his 1996 book of the same name.[3] Goleman believes that emotional literacy is as important as intellectual ability, and that the social and emotional aspects of how leaders work make or break their impact.

In a nutshell, emotional intelligence is really PEOPLE intelligence—the ability to 1) understand your own emotional landscape and 2) engage with others productively.

The order matters. First, understand yourself, and then you will be on more solid footing in your relationships with others. Without the capacity to recognize and navigate your own emotions, it is unlikely that you will be able to engage well with a coworker's emotional reality.

In the Harvard Business Review article "What Makes a Leader?"[4] Goleman outlines the five components of emotional intelligence: self-awareness, self-regulation, motivation, empathy and social skill. The degree to which a person masters these competencies impacts the types of choices made and the impact of those choices on other people and what can be accomplished by the team.

People making choices that evidence high PEOPLE orientation are adaptive, and they maintain a real-time sense of the emotional realities of others. They are able to influence others, be agents for change when needed, and navigate the complexities of working together with other emotional beings.

Low EQ may be evidenced by a limited emotional vocabulary, a lack of anger when it may even be justified (stifling negative emotions) or lack of assertiveness. A team member with low EQ may find it

---

3   Goleman, D., *Emotional Intelligence: Why It Can Matter More than IQ*. New York: Bantam Books, 1995.

4   Goleman, D., "What Makes a Leader?" *Harvard Business Review*, 76 (6) (1998): 93-102.

CHAPTER 2: LEADERSHIP, TEAMWORK, AND CHOICE

hard to connect with others on a personal level, which negatively impacts employee engagement and motivation. Working through tough problems at work can be made even more difficult without an understanding of the self or others' emotional state. Though a lack of emotional intelligence can appear as harshness, many people don't intend to be dismissive. They simply don't think about considering the people aspects of their work.

A person making low PEOPLE choices may have a desire to seek a greater-good solution. They may even be highly committed and willing to work tirelessly to make a positive impact. However, if they lack self-awareness or an ability to understand or relate to others, their choices will be different—and have different outcomes—from a person with high EQ.

That does not mean that a person with a high EQ will always orient toward what is best for the greater good. Indeed, individuals with high emotional intelligence can skillfully use their people skills to advance their own self-interest, without regard for others.

> Worried about a person who uses emotional intelligence for less-than-noble purposes? Check out this article on Inc.com: "10 Ways Manipulators Use Emotional Intelligence for Evil (and How to Fight Back)." https://www.inc.com/justin-bariso/10-ways-manipulators-use-emotional-intelligence-for-evil-and-how-to-fight-back.html

Likewise, high EQ may or may not correlate with high COMMITMENT. A person may be highly self-aware and possess people skills, yet not have the sustained enthusiasm and COMMITMENT to make things happen. They may be well-calibrated emotionally and engage productively with others. Yet they lack the persistence and drive to hang in there when things get difficult.

> Not sure about your level of emotional intelligence (EQ)? Check out this article by Dr. Travis Bradberry on "Eleven Signs That You Lack Emotional Intelligence." https://www.linkedin.com/pulse/eleven-signs-you-lack-emotional-intelligence-dr-travis-bradberry/

CHOICES OF LEADERSHIP: PUTTING IT ALL TOGETHER

Layering in emotional intelligence (EQ) rounds out the picture of the types of choices individuals make.

These eight choices combine all three elements of leadership choices—CARE (greater good/self), the degree of COMMITMENT to impact, and PEOPLE (emotional intelligence or EQ) (Figure 2).

Consider the example of the soccer team parents who have the job of taking down the goal nets after each practice and game. The different types of choices are summarized in Figure 3.

CHOICES AT WORK

There are an infinite number of scenarios at work where the choices play out, but one of the most common is meetings. Whenever you bring people together, their choices combine to create conflict, chaos or collaboration. The choice is everyone's. Here are how the 8 Choices of Leadership play out at meetings.

Consider the impact of the types of choices people make in meetings. How much would be accomplished if most people operated in the transformative or productive space? If meeting attendees are choosing behaviors in the bottom half (passive, destructive, submissive or manipulative), how might the outcomes of the meeting be different?

Daily choices impact the people and organizations in which they occur. Sometimes the effects are trivial. In other situations, individual choices can mean the difference between a safe work environment and one that puts people at risk, potentially endangering people's lives.

CHAPTER 2: LEADERSHIP, TEAMWORK, AND CHOICE

One arena in which choices can be a matter of critical importance (even life or death) is safety issues in a manufacturing plant.

> A McKinsey study identified four kinds of behavior that account for 89 percent of leadership effectiveness. These include more "COMMITMENT-oriented" behaviors, like "operate with strong results orientation" and "solve problems effectively." The article also pointed to PEOPLE behaviors as a driver of effectiveness ("be supportive"). Inclusive, greater-good CARE behaviors like "seek different perspectives" also lead to success.[5]

When you think about individuals and teams, achieving greatness isn't simply a matter of doing a certain list of functions. To get the maximum impact, people at all levels must be committed to achieve the right things (COMMITMENT to impact) for the right reasons (CARE for greater good) and in the right ways (PEOPLE intelligence).

We call the combination of CARE, COMMITMENT and PEOPLE the Green Path. Consistently making choices of this nature creates great teams and makes a great impact in the world. We will explore more about the paths in Chapter 4. First, how do individuals and teams change the types of daily choices they make?

---

[5] Feser, C., F. Mayol, and R. Srinivasan, "Decoding Leadership: What Really Matters." *McKinsey Quarterly.* (January 2015) Retrieved from https://www.mckinsey.com/global-themes/leadership/decoding-leadership-what-really-matters

8 CHOICES OF LEADERSHIP

PRODUCTIVE (High greater good focus, low commitment to impact, high understanding of people)	**TRANSFORMATIVE** (High greater good focus, high commitment to impact, high understanding of people)	HIGH EQ
SLACKTIVE (High greater good focus, low commitment to impact, low understanding of people)	**DIRECTIVE** (High greater good focus, high commitment to impact, low understanding of people)	LOW EQ
PASSIVE (Low greater good focus, low commitment to impact, low understanding of people)	**DESTRUCTIVE** (Low greater good focus, high commitment to impact, low understanding of people)	
SUBMISSIVE (Low greater good focus, low commitment to impact, high understanding of people)	**MANIPULATIVE** (Low greater good focus, high commitment to impact, high understanding of people)	HIGH EQ
COMFORT	COMMITMENT → IMPACT	

GREATER GOOD ← CARE / SELF

PEOPLE →

Figure 2

8 CHOICES OF LEADERSHIP

	CARE →	
SELF		GREATER GOOD

PRODUCTIVE
When asked, will help take down nets with a positive attitude.

SLACKTIVE
Talks about how they will help, how important helping is, and identifies how others aren't pulling their weight, but often doesn't actually do anything.

PASSIVE
Hangs around and avoids doing anything.

SUBMISSIVE
Reluctantly does what others directly ask them to do, but without enthusiasm or interest.

TRANSFORMATIVE
Coordinates and engages parents to take nets down so that they are ready for the next game.

DIRECTIVE
Orders others to help take nets down.

DESTRUCTIVE
Heads to referee, finger cocked and loaded, ready to give the referee a piece of their mind as to how the last call destroyed their six-year-old's chances of playing in the World Cup. Ignores issue of net as not important.

MANIPULATIVE
Gets others to complain about the organization, take the nets down, and then give their kids a ride home.

COMFORT ← COMMITMENT → IMPACT

HIGH EQ / LOW EQ / HIGH EQ

PEOPLE →

Figure 3

CHAPTER 3: CHANGING CHOICES

ARE CHOICES REALLY A CHOICE?

THE PROJECT GOES BADLY, and everyone begins the blame game.

The boss is in a terrible mood and yells at everyone. They, in turn, become frustrated with minor problems exhibited by their direct reports.

Daily choices can feel like they are not in the person's control. The truth is, every person chooses every behavior every day, even if they are not consciously aware of it.

> "The difference between who you are and who you want to be is what you do." Charles Duhigg, author of *The Power of Habit: Why We Do What We Do in Life and Business*

How do you get out of autopilot mode and change the default choice you make?

KNOW YOURSELF

To change a habit, first figure out what it is, when you do it and why it's part of your life. Charles Duhigg's 2012 book, *The Power of*

Habit: Why We Do What We Do in Life and Business[6], describes the three aspects of habits:

1. Cue—What triggers you to do the habitual behavior (e.g., waking up)
2. Routine—Your automatic behaviors associated with that cue (e.g., preparing and drinking coffee)
3. Reward—What you get from doing the routine (e.g., smell, taste and energy boost)

Brains love rewards, and that's how the habit is reinforced whenever the routine follows the cue. If you've ever tried to change a bad habit, like eating junk food, through sheer willpower, you understand that it's not that simple.

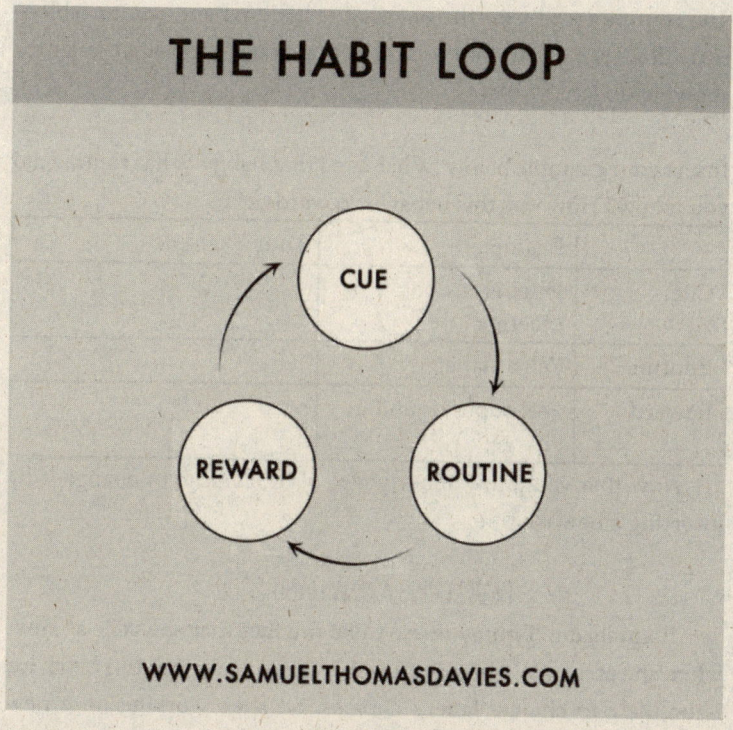

---
6 Duhigg, Charles. *The Power of Habit: Why We Do What We Do in Life and Business*. New York: Random House, 2012. Print.

Habits play a huge role in teamwork and the choices people make. Think about your work with others. What choice have you made recently that you wish you could do over? These regretted choices are clues about the habitual ways you behave that can cause problems in your team. Did you blow up at a colleague when he made a mistake? Avoid a conflictual conversation that you really needed to have? Micromanage others in order to get things done your way?

HABIT LOOP AND CHANGING CHOICES

Once again, the meeting is fifteen minutes underway, and in walks Janet. The team leader, Tammy, reacts without giving it much thought, blowing off steam that has been building up for months. The routine response—the one that is habitual and comfortable—is to allow the frustration to take center stage and yell at Janet for showing up late.

Insert your example below. What cued that habit? What routine did you follow? How was this behavior rewarded?

	Example	Your Example
Cue	Janet is late to meeting	
Routine	Yell at Janet	
Reward	Feel superior and in charge	

Now that you know about your habit, it's time to change it by inserting a new routine.

DEVELOPING A NEW HABIT LOOP

Team leader Tammy doesn't like the fact that she yells at Janet when she arrives late to meetings. She also knows that this behavior is unlikely to change Janet's choices. So she's working on a new routine response.

	Example	Your Example
Cue	Janet is late to meeting	
Routine	Continue meeting and engage Janet in private to understand and agree on expectations	
Reward	Satisfaction of getting meeting goals accomplished and building relationship and accountability with Janet	

Notice that the only thing that has changed is the way Tammy reacts when Janet was late. That creates a different reward, and that reward will have an impact on how the cue affects Tammy in the future. Janet may indeed be late for another meeting. Tammy cannot control that. What she can control is how she reacts if this happens. And that new choice sets the stage for a whole different (and better) set of outcomes—less meeting distraction, pride in modeling the right behavior for the team, etc.

CIMA: FOUR QUESTIONS TO CALIBRATE AND MAKE BETTER CHOICES

When a machine is not calibrated, it breaks down over time. When we are not calibrated with the world around us, we don't always make choices we are proud of. Not only do we fail to work together to achieve team goals, we also act in ways that negatively impact our relationships. Either we become too frustrated in situations and lose our cool, or we throw our hands up and simply stop trying. Neither will produce a desired outcome of mutual support, influence and achieving shared goals. Working with others requires constantly calibrating to the world around you, and even more so in situations where the outcome is important.

One way to calibrate is the Serenity Prayer: "Grant me the serenity to accept the things that I cannot change, the courage to change the things that I can, AND the wisdom to know the difference." It basically says life is broken down into two buckets: you either control it or you don't. For that which we don't control (which is everything except us!), there are a couple other buckets to add beyond just having to accept it—you can influence it and/or you can manage for it.

Here are four questions to ask yourself so that you can calibrate to reality and then produce the best possible outcome.

Question 1: What do I Control? Sometimes we attempt to control things we can't—like others' attitudes, work habits, decisions, and their perspectives. In reality, the only thing we control is us—our own thoughts, our attitudes and our choices. Put the wrong things in this bucket and you will become overly frustrated and lose credibility. You do not control others; you control you—period.

Question 2: Who/what do I Influence? Influence is often based upon the quality of your connection with others. In the book *Speed of Trust*, Covey discusses that trust is earned through character (integrity and motives) and competency (skills and results). Invest in building the bank account with others by consistently demonstrating the right character and that you are competent. Work hard to understand the WIIFM (What's In It For Me?) of whoever you are trying to influence, and choose to see the world through their eyes. Reciprocation is one key influencer—honestly ask yourself, when have you been open to the other person's influence or point of view?

Question 3: How can I Mitigate the risk or exposure in this situation? There are some factors we cannot control or influence, so we must ensure that we mitigate them. This simply means lessening the impact. This is done through being proactive. For example, if you know that someone might be initially resistant to an idea, talk with them about the idea a few days prior to the meeting that you're having with all the stakeholders. There's a saying: "Involve me early, I'll be your partner; involve me late, I'll be your judge." Another way to mitigate the impact of someone who is generally negative is to plan your responses ahead of time so that you do not allow your buttons to be pushed. While you may not be able to influence them to change, you will gain credibility by responding rather than reacting to them.

Question 4: What must I **A**ccept? Lastly, there are some things we simply need to accept. These are all of the things we cannot control, influence or mitigate. This is where we simply must "let things go" and not let it drain our time and energy. Caution: don't put things too quickly in this bucket and just give up.

PAY ATTENTION

Many of our daily choices happen without our conscious awareness. How can you pay better attention to those choices and habits so that you can actively decide on your behavior?

Paying attention seems like a simple answer. Yet in the hustle and bustle of life, it is not easy to do. However, if we tune in to what is going on around us and within us, we stand a much better chance of exercising sound judgment around behavior.

There are many strategies for being more aware on a moment-by-moment basis. One technique is a four-step process: notice, stop, think, choose.

1. Notice: First, tune in and recognize how you're feeling. How is your body reacting? Pay attention to the clues your body is giving you.
2. Stop: Create a choice space by not reacting right away. Breathe. Count to ten. Grab a notepad and pen so you can buy yourself a few moments. Cup one hand in another hand as a physical reminder to be centered before reacting.
3. Think: Where is my CARE now? Am I strongly committed to impact (COMMITMENT)? Am I aware of my own emotions and those of others (PEOPLE)? How can I best make a choice that keeps the greater good, impact and relationships as the focus?
4. Choose: Now that you are able to decide how to behave, make a choice that demonstrates your CARE for others (as well as

self), high COMMITMENT to impact, and strong PEOPLE (emotional) intelligence.

Another tool for paying better attention is journaling—creating a regular practice of reflection and writing.

Research has shown that journaling has positive physical and mental health benefits, like reducing stress. Writing your thoughts and feelings can also help you solve problems and achieve goals.

Journaling promotes self-awareness and an opportunity to think more deeply about important issues, choices and behavior. Regular journaling helps the writer see progress (or lack thereof) over time. Journaling can also help individuals be more present later on. The process of journaling sets people up to be more aware of their thinking and emotions in the moment, able to choose actions and understand the likely impact of those behaviors on others.

Some people have used a Daily Choices journal, focusing specifically on some of the choices they made that day, how they came about, and the ripple effects of those chosen behaviors. This provides an opportunity to reflect on where in the 8 Choices (see Chapter 2) those behaviors fell, and to create a plan to make more transformative choices in the future.

BOOST PEOPLE SKILLS (EMOTIONAL INTELLIGENCE, EI OR EQ)

One of the most challenging aspects of choice is PEOPLE or emotional intelligence. Emotional intelligence affects how individuals manage their behaviors, navigate social interactions and relationships, and make personal decisions. Otherwise intelligent, thoughtful people can struggle with understanding and managing their own emotional state and dealing with the feelings of others.

First, let's get some clarity about the basics of emotions and feelings. Though we often use them interchangeably in conversation (and in this book), there is a distinct difference between feelings and emotions.

Neurologist Antonio R. Damasio was quoted in *Scientific*

American, stating that "emotions are more or less the complex reactions the body has to certain stimuli. When we are afraid of something, our hearts begin to race, our mouths become dry, our skin turns pale and our muscles contract. This emotional reaction occurs automatically and unconsciously."[7]

Dr. Damasio goes on to define feelings, which come after the emotions and unconscious physical reactions. "Feelings occur after we become aware in our brain of such physical changes; only then do we experience the feeling of fear."

STIMULUS→EMOTION→PHYSICAL REACTION→FEELINGS→THOUGHTS

Because the brain processes inputs through the limbic (emotional) system first, before any rational thought, humans experience emotions before thinking. Thankfully, when they pay attention, humans can recognize their emotions, physical reactions and subsequent feelings. They can get better at deciding what thoughts they will dwell upon as well.

> Travis Bradberry and Jean Greaves isolate four aspects of emotional intelligence in their practical book, *Emotional Intelligence 2.0*. They define emotional intelligence as the "ability to recognize and understand emotions in yourself and others, and your ability to use this awareness to manage your behavior and relationships."[8]

Some find emotions—even their own—to be mysterious, complex or unpleasant. Perhaps their families did not recognize or acknowledge feelings, so they never became conversant with understanding or naming emotions or feelings. And if a person cannot recognize their own feelings or assign a meaning to them, it is very difficult to navigate the emotions of others.

---

[7] Lenzen, M. (2005, April 1) *Scientific American Mind*. Feeling Our Emotions. Retrieved from https://www.scientificamerican.com/article/feeling-our-emotions/
[8] Bradberry, T., & Greaves, J. (2009). *Emotional intelligence 2.0*. San Diego, CA: TalentSmart.

> "Only 36 percent of the people we tested are able to accurately identify their emotions as they happen."[9]

Emotions at work can be especially fraught. In most workplaces, expressing strong emotion can be seen as a lack of control or sign of weakness: "Wow, Sue really flew off the handle" or "Can you believe Alexander cried at that meeting?"

Coming to terms with emotions—yours and others'—is an integral part of teamwork. Emotions are real and impact individuals and teams. We all have them. One reason why we struggle to manage emotions is that we do not understand their nature, where they come from, and what can be done about them.

We often use the 4 Cs of Leadership in reference to many competencies, and they are particularly useful when considering emotional intelligence. Use this to gauge where you are in terms of EI, and seek feedback and coaching to improve.

THE 4 CS OF EMOTIONAL INTELLIGENCE

Level	Description	✓
Clueless	I don't get emotions at all	☐
Clone	I understand myself and assume everyone's emotional landscape is just like mine	☐
Categorical	I have some understanding based on the labels, but it is oversimplified and may be based on stereotypes	☐
Customized	I understand my own emotions and have good methods for reading and reacting to others' as well	☐

Bradberry and Greaves, who developed the ideas behind emotional intelligence, break it down into four quadrants:

---

9   Ibid

EMOTIONAL INTELLIGENCE	What I see	What I do
Personal Competence	Self-awareness	Self-management
Social Competence	Social awareness	Relationship management

Emotional Intelligence 2.0 provides sixty-six strategies for boosting emotional intelligence. They recommend choosing one of the four quadrants above to focus on, choosing a short list (one to three) of strategies to practice, and finding a mentor—someone who is skilled at the area you're trying to improve.

Some sample strategies for each quadrant:

Quadrant	Sample Strategies
Self-awareness	• Quit treating your feelings as good or bad • Feel your emotions physically; pay attention to body cues • Know who and what pushes your buttons • Spot emotions in books, movies and music
Social awareness	• Greet people by name • Be mindful; live in the moment • Practice the art of listening • Seek the whole picture, including others' ideas and emotions
Self-management	• Breathe right (slowly and deeply) • Count to ten • Take control of your self-talk • Put a mental recharge into your schedule (and do it)
Relationship management	• Be open and be curious • Take feedback well • Don't avoid the inevitable, even if there is conflict • When you care, show it

Emotional intelligence sets people up to make better moment-by-moment choices. It is important to both challenge yourself to improve as it relates to EI, while extending your self-compassion as well. When you're tempted to be hard on yourself (*Why did I just yell at my kids?!*), imagine that a close friend had just done the same thing. How would you show compassion in that situation? Extend the same compassionate response to yourself, while holding yourself accountable to do better next time.

Remember that the heat of the moment is not the time to start working on emotional intelligence. Practice using emotional intelligence at times and in situations that are not quite as intense. That will embed a more fluid habit that will prepare you to make a better choice when emotions run high.

IMPROVE COMMITMENT (TO IMPACT)

What do you do if you recognize that you're not as committed or dedicated to your team's work as you'd like to be? You may be missing deadlines or not working with intensity. You could feel drawn to comfortable routines or schedules. You may not feel able to muster the same enthusiasm you had in the past or that you see others on the team exhibit.

If you find you are not making choices based on a strong COMMITMENT to impact, consider one of these strategies:

1. Start new. Tell yourself that today is your first day in this effort. How do you want to be present? How can you make a difference? (Fresh starts are not reserved for New Year's Day.)

2. Consider fit with your preferences, values and purpose. Maybe this work (or volunteer role) is not one you're excited about, so true COMMITMENT is not really there. If you find that you can't wait to help out at your child's school, but you find it difficult to summon much enthusiasm about your accounting job, maybe you've made a bad career choice. (Or maybe you just haven't spent enough time in that classroom, so it feels fresh and

new.) Some honest soul-searching may reveal that even though that big promotion seemed exciting, you don't really enjoy the pressure or long hours. Yes, switching jobs or even career fields is hard. Sticking with something you are not passionate about is not sustainable. Over time, your happiness and results will both suffer.

3. Take care of you. Maybe you can't give the PTA chair role as much energy as you would like because you're sleeping three hours a night, have a chronic health problem or are eating Doritos all day every day. Overhaul your self-care, and you may find that your COMMITMENT is all in.

CAN YOU CHANGE CARE (GREATER GOOD OR SELF ONLY)?

The three aspects of all of our choices—CARE (greater good v. self only), COMMITMENT to impact and PEOPLE (emotional intelligence)—are reflected in the types of behaviors we exhibit. So what can be done about amping up CARE for the greater good? Can a person who is essentially self-focused learn to shift to a greater-good perspective?

There are degrees of self-orientation, ranging from a tendency toward self-centeredness to narcissism. According to the Mayo Clinic, narcissistic personality disorder is a mental condition in which people have an inflated sense of their own importance, a deep need for excessive attention and admiration, troubled relationships, and a lack of empathy for others. A narcissist, often a master manipulator of others, would make a very challenging team member, one who is unlikely to be influenced to change. However, there are some strategies that may be employed.

This advice from *Harvard Business Review*'s Manfred F. R. Kets de Vries ("How to Manage a Narcissist") can be applied to productively work with a self-centered person as well.

1. Use strong team engagement. A cohesive team will be able to call out unacceptable behavior and take the focus off the one

person giving the feedback. This peer pressure can help the narcissist to look at the problematic behaviors.

2. Create a safe, somewhat playful work culture. This will encourage openness, communication and exploration of behaviors.

3. Support the team in confronting problematic behaviors of the narcissist. Empowered peers will have more impact than an enforcing boss.

For those working on a team with a self-oriented person (we'll call him self-absorbed Sam), the best advice we can give is to not let Sam influence your choices. Limit the influence and impact of Sam's choices on others. If these strategies do not work, consider whether Sam should continue as a member of the team.

CHAPTER 4: CHOICES AND PROCESSES

INTRODUCTION TO PATHS

TEAMWORK IS A COMPOSITE of the moment-by-moment *choices* of people and the *processes* that are necessary to get things done. We have covered a lot of information on individual choices, and how they impact others. Now it is time to look at the processes, the "doing," of great teams.

The required processes of teamwork include *set up the team, plan work, do work* and (inevitably) *wrestle with issues*. (These processes will be explored further later in this chapter.) How well teams perform these functions is largely determined by the combined qualities of their choices. Together, this composite of the individuals' choices is called a path.

Here's the "What Great Teams Do Great" model (Figure 4). The path teams take (denoted by green and red arrows) are either predominantly red or green at any given time.

When (not if) things don't go 100 percent as planned, teams use cycles that either help them recover (green) or put them on a path to failure (red).

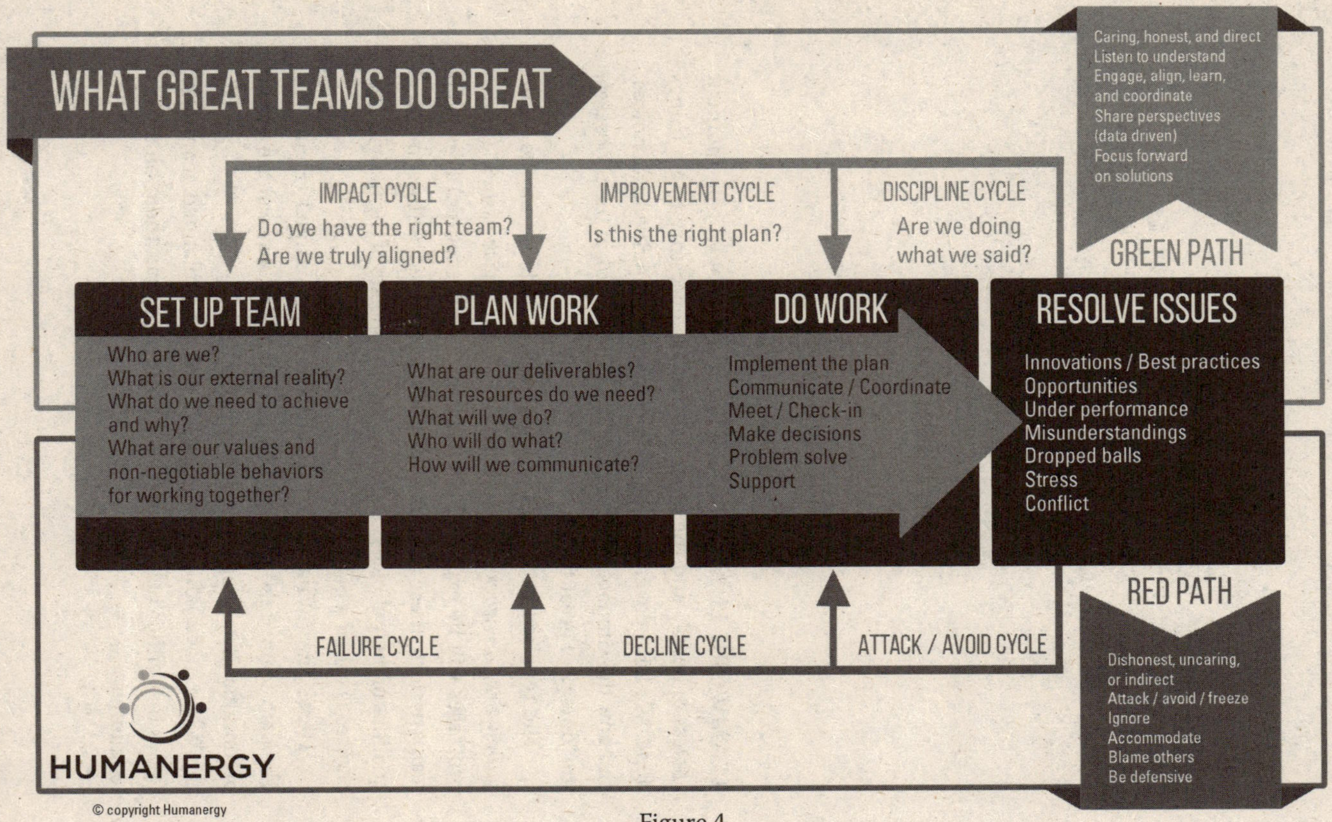

WHAT GREAT TEAMS DO GREAT

GREEN PATH
- Caring, honest, and direct
- Listen to understand
- Engage, align, learn and coordinate
- Share perspectives (data driven)
- Focus forward on solutions

RED PATH
- Dishonest, uncaring, or indirect
- Attack / avoid / freeze
- Ignore
- Accommodate
- Blame others
- Be defensive

SET UP TEAM
- Who are we?
- What is our external reality?
- What do we need to achieve and why?
- What are our values and non-negotiable behaviors for working together?

PLAN WORK
- What are our deliverables?
- What resources do we need?
- What will we do?
- Who will do what?
- How will we communicate?

DO WORK
- Implement the plan
- Communicate / Coordinate
- Meet / Check-in
- Make decisions
- Problem solve
- Support

RESOLVE ISSUES
- Innovations / Best practices
- Opportunities
- Under performance
- Misunderstandings
- Dropped balls
- Stress
- Conflict

IMPACT CYCLE — Do we have the right team? Are we truly aligned?

IMPROVEMENT CYCLE — Is this the right plan?

DISCIPLINE CYCLE — Are we doing what we said?

FAILURE CYCLE · DECLINE CYCLE · ATTACK / AVOID CYCLE

HUMANERGY
© copyright Humanergy

Figure 4

HOW PATHS WORK

Think of a choice by an individual team member as a single brick in this path.

For simplicity's sake, we categorize choices as green or red (though, of course, there are degrees of intensity of redness and green-ness). Again, green choices are ones that are high in CARE for greater good, COMMITMENT to impact and PEOPLE (emotional intelligence).

As team members make choices throughout the days/weeks/months, the "path" becomes colored with many bricks.

This path—a composite of team choices—determines how well the team performs every aspect of team processes. This collective set of behaviors will help the team set up the team, plan work, do the work, resolve issues, and hopefully create successful outcomes. Or not.

The team's daily, moment-by-moment choices, and the thinking behind them, can also be thought of as the team's culture. By focusing on team members' individual choices, a team (and on a larger scale, the organization) can shift its culture in the direction of continuous improvement and consistently achieving excellence in a changing and challenging world. The more team members take the Green Path, the more they influence and contribute to the "green" culture.

And, in a virtuous cycle, the more often team members take the Green Path, the easier it is to take the Green Path in the future. Even in difficult situations, people become more fluid and habitual in their use of Green Path choices.

A great team will not have all green choices. Even a Green Path always has some red bricks in it. (Team members are human and will make red choices from time to time.) However, teams making daily green choices are much better equipped to achieve success and do so with much less hassle and strife.

Teams may dip into a predominantly Red Path for a period of time. That provides a ripe choice space. Do they continue to spiral further into the Red Path, losing focus on their goals and practicing behaviors that fracture the team? Or do they weather the storm and find strength in the midst of adversity? Some teams find that recovering from a period of less-than-stellar performance actually makes them stronger in the long term. They acknowledge the practices that did not serve them well, create new norms for behavior, and move forward. Seeing the opportunity that lies within difficulties is a hallmark of a great team.

> *"The world breaks everyone and afterward many are strong at the broken places."*
> —Ernest Hemingway

What are the team behaviors involved in a Green Path?
- Caring, honest and direct communication
- Listen to understand
- Engage, align, learn and coordinate
- Share perspectives (data driven)
- Focus forward on solutions

In contrast, Red Path behaviors include:
- Dishonest, uncaring or indirect communication
- Attack/Avoid/Freeze
- Ignore
- Accommodate
- Blame others
- Be defensive

Simply stating "We're going to do Green Path behaviors" isn't going to guarantee team greatness. There must be deliberate, ongoing efforts to ensure that the team stays on the "green side."

BOOSTING GREEN PATH COMPETENCY

To keep the team operating on the Green Path, it is vital to devote time and energy to the critical competencies required for greatness. Teams must 1) *anticipate* challenges and scenarios that will trigger Red Path mode, 2) *prepare* their responses and 3) *practice* the Green Path behaviors regularly. This *anticipate/prepare/practice* regimen will build resiliency in the team and help them be ready for issues that will arise.

How do teams develop Green Path choices and behaviors? Caring, honest and direct communication. It can be difficult to confront uncomfortable situations in any group. Teams often struggle to communicate, and this is more of a problem if members sense conflict around a particular issue. In these situations, some people will engage early and others may wait until they get angry to say anything. Others avoid conflictual topics at any cost.

Unfortunately, not dealing with conflict early on makes the problems larger and more difficult to solve. This results in a phenomenon we call the "slippery slope" (Figure 5).

THE SLIPPERY SLOPE

Choosing the Green Path means being proactive and engaging with others when an issue needs to be addressed. Unfortunately, this is often not the most common way of dealing with conflict. Many people will admit, "I just don't like conflict!" They may use the excuse "Oh, Bob is just like that. It's not a big deal." In some cases it may be a big deal. And Bob isn't going to change without some type of communication, at a minimum.

The danger of the slippery slope is that tension continues to build. Before the team knows it, they are in a very destructive zone, engaging in behaviors that are solidly on the Red Path. This has made

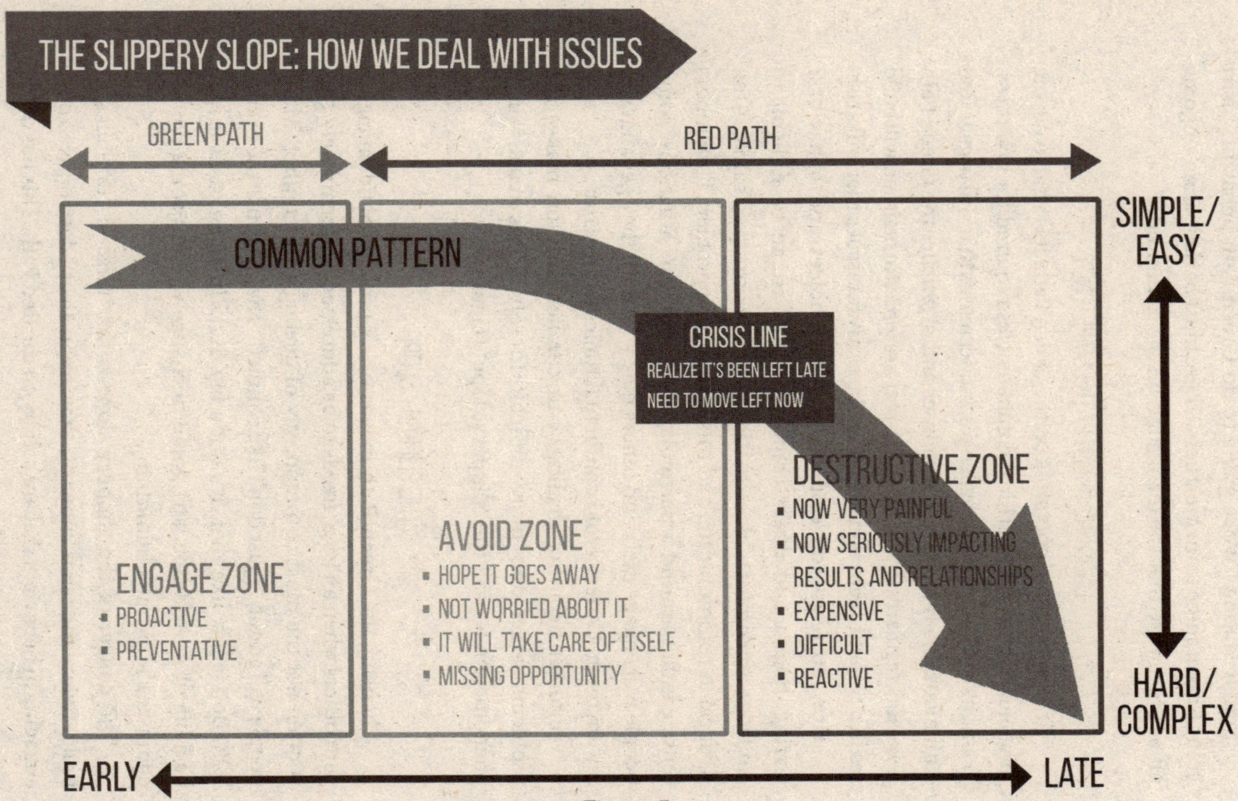
THE SLIPPERY SLOPE: HOW WE DEAL WITH ISSUES
GREEN PATH
RED PATH
COMMON PATTERN
CRISIS LINE
REALIZE IT'S BEEN LEFT LATE
NEED TO MOVE LEFT NOW
ENGAGE ZONE
PROACTIVE
PREVENTATIVE
AVOID ZONE
HOPE IT GOES AWAY
NOT WORRIED ABOUT IT
IT WILL TAKE CARE OF ITSELF
MISSING OPPORTUNITY
DESTRUCTIVE ZONE
NOW VERY PAINFUL
NOW SERIOUSLY IMPACTING RESULTS AND RELATIONSHIPS
EXPENSIVE
DIFFICULT
REACTIVE
SIMPLE/ EASY
HARD/ COMPLEX
EARLY
LATE

Figure 5

the original problem bigger and more complex. Festering conflict makes every interaction and task more difficult than it needs to be. Over time, progress on the work at hand will begin to be affected.

Avoid the slippery slope by engaging early in caring, honest and direct communication.

TRANSFORMATIVE DISCUSSIONS

To engage in caring, honest and direct communication, many teams have found value in a process called transformative discussions (Figure 6). The focus of a transformative discussion is progress on the issue, not winning an argument or scoring points. The conversation must be approached with a mindset of CARE, safety, and the greater good of the team. Approaching a difficult topic with a mindset of CARE for everyone and everything impacted by the issue sets you up for finding win-win solutions.

Yes, the process looks complicated. And we will break it down into manageable chunks.

First, begin with some important preparation. Focus first on your own mindset coming into the discussion. Use this table to increase self-awareness, align on what must be achieved regarding the topic and to maintain the relationship, and summarize what is understood about the situation before going into the conversation.

TRANSFORMATIVE GREEN PATH

STEPS	FIRST ME	THEN US
1. SELF/OTHER UNDERSTANDING	What are my "red path" stories? My baggage? My self-justifications?	Be aware NOT to be pulled into attack, avoid, blame, defensiveness, accommodating behaviors
2. GREATER GOOD	What is best for me, other, and our relationship?	State intent of forward focus for the greater good.
3. CARE AND SAFETY	Remember I am working with a person, not a problem. I control myself and I might influence the other person.	Show care for other; make it safe as possible.
4. MUTUAL UNDERSTANDING	How well do I understand the situation? What is my story, feelings, facts, opinions, assumptions, and role?	"Help me understand." Summerize regularly— "What I understand is..."
5. COMMON GROUND	What common ground might we share?	"AND we agree that..."
6. EXPANDED GROUND	What is important information necessary to resolve the situation?	"AND we need to know that..."
7. RESOLVE DIFFERENCES	What do I need to say to be caring, honest, and direct?	"AND our difference appears to be..."
8. GREATER GOOD SOLUTION		"AND let us work out how we can move forward together."

Figure 6

TRANSFORMATIVE DISCUSSIONS WORKSHEET: PRE-DISCUSSION

1. Recognize "Red Path" stories What is my baggage? What are my self-justifications to • Avoid, ignore or accommodate? • Attack, blame or be defensive?	
2. What are WE trying to achieve and why? What is best for me, the other and our relationship? 3. How can I make the discussion as safe as possible?	
4. What is the issue from my perspective? • Accept my own feelings 5. How well do I understand the situation? • What are the facts? What are my opinions? • What are my assumptions? • What part have I played in the issue?	
6. What common ground might we share? 7. What will it look like to be : • Direct • Honest • Caring	

When the necessary preparation has happened, use the following worksheet to guide the transformative discussion itself. The focus here is to create an atmosphere of safety and CARE, achieve mutual understanding, and create lasting solutions that are for the greater good.

You will notice a number of "ANDs" in this process. Using "AND" counteracts the typical response of "yes, but..." (or simply "but") that characterizes many difficult conversations. Using "AND" recognizes that people can agree on many things without discounting those alignments with a "but."

TRANSFORMATIVE DISCUSSIONS WORKSHEET: DURING THE DISCUSSION

1. Self/Other understanding 2. State intent as forward focus for greater good (what WE are trying to achieve and why) 3. Show care for the other, making it as safe as possible 4. State the issue in a way that is clear, concise and can be heard by the other	
5. Listen and show understanding throughout • Share perspectives; use "and," not "but" • Use "help me understand" when unsure • Summarize regularly ("what I understand is...") • How does the other see the issue? 6. What do we have in common? ("AND we agree that...") 7. What are our differences? ("AND our differences appear to be...")	
8. Greater-good solution ("AND let us work out how we can move forward together.")	

LISTEN TO UNDERSTAND

When it comes to achieving mutual understanding, we have a listening crisis. Too many people listen with an agenda to make a judgment, build their own counter-argument or simply wait out the other person's speaking. In fact, as Margaret Millar said, "most conversations are simply monologues delivered in the presence of a witness."

There are up to five steps that may be necessary in order to listen well. Steps one through three, at a minimum, allow the listener to truly hear what the speaker is conveying.

1. Listen to absorb meaning. This requires suspending the listener's thoughts, categorizations, preferences, judgments and agenda.
2. Pay attention to the nonverbals—body language, tone of voice, facial expression, etc.
3. Close the loop. This step involves briefly summarizing what the speaker has said. Rather than parroting back the same words, simply state the core meaning you feel the speaker is trying to express.
4. Ask clarifying questions, if needed. (You may not have gotten the full intent and content of the message in your first summary.)
5. Close the loop again, if necessary.

Complete listening is rare in modern society, and it is a gift to both the speaker and the listener. It allows the listener to value the speaker and absorb what the speaker is saying. The speaker is valued and heard, something that is shockingly rare in modern discourse.

In a discussion aimed at mutual understanding, it is important for all parties to be heard fully. Once the listener understands the perspective of the speaker, the listener can then switch roles and begin speaking.

Listening to understand does not mean that the listener agrees or will agree with everything the speaker is saying. This full listening habit, however, allows for mutual understanding of varying perspectives that may come together to form innovative solutions down the road.

ENGAGE, ALIGN, LEARN AND COORDINATE

Entire books have been written about how teams come together to engage, align, learn and coordinate their actions for a common purpose. We will briefly break down each of these four team practices to understand how great teams become and stay great.

Engage. The Merriam-Webster definition of the word "engage" is multifaceted. So too is engagement among team members. Some of the definitions, like "to interlock with" or "to deal with especially at length" or "to begin and carry on an enterprise or activity" align well with what teams do. They must interact and bring their various skills together to achieve their stated goals.

Engagement as a team is not easy or without peril. Indeed, the definition "to expose to risk for the attainment or support of some end" applies very well to engagement in teamwork.

Teams don't have to strive for complete unity or groupthink. Great teams know when to let individual differences be a driving force for innovation. Likewise, they know how and when to intervene when a team member loses focus or needs increased accountability. They find the right balance between individual freedom and responsibility for shared outcomes.

Align. Getting on the same page means that the team knows what results and impact are expected and understands the parameters on how to get there. Alignment is not something a great team can get once and then forget about. All alignment has a shelf life, as we've said before. Great teams are motivated to achieve their purpose, and they recognize the signs of misalignment early, taking bold steps to refocus and move forward.

Alignment does not mean simply getting people to comply or agree for the good of the team. Great teams not only share goals, but they also find ways to ensure that these goals inspire passion and commitment.

Learn. No great team or great team member has ever truly "arrived." They recognize that every person on the team must continue growth and learning over time. Great teams seek out opportunities to continue learning through formal training, mentorship, sharing of resources, and intentional continuous improvement processes.

Sometimes learning happens best when things go wrong. Great teams understand that mistakes and problems are opportunities for improvement. They make sure to learn from both the things that go well and the problems that occur.

Coordinate. Teamwork = 100 percent collaboration at all times, right? No. One of the reasons people find teamwork so difficult is that they actually collaborate too much. Great teams know when and how they should coordinate their resources, bringing others in when it's needed. Exceptional teams know when it is best to "divide and conquer" as well. The "Sweet Spot of Collaboration" is a tool great teams use to make sure they are working at the right level of coordination.

SWEET SPOT OF COLLABORATION

Teams need the whole team involved with alignment on major aspects of the work, like vision, mission and what the team is accountable for (Figure 7).

Smaller work teams can be utilized when the work is complex, requires multiple skill sets, or would benefit from creative input. In those situations, there is great potential for a group of three to five people to bring real synergy and added value to the work. All other work of the team is largely individual, especially when adding other perspectives would simply bog down the process or not add value.

Share perspectives (data driven). Every team is composed of plenty of opinions. Great teams certainly contain opinionated people as well, but they know that it is important to consider the facts behind the situations the team faces. How teams share perspectives around issues varies. Sometimes it's one-way communication, like via email, when information needs to be shared without input. However, great teams recognize that when the matter is important, they need to get input from a wide variety of team members. And not everyone feels comfortable sharing their positions in a large group setting. Some may prefer a more discreet setting or might need time for contemplation before chiming in with their thoughts. Great teams do what needs to be done to garner diverse perspectives on the important issues. They customize sharing and receiving input to meet the needs of the situation and of the individual team members.

Focus forward on solutions. Experiences from the past can be highly instructive when it comes to learning. However, great teams focus most of their energy and passion on the future, rather than ruminating about what occurred before. When problems happen, even great teams may momentarily be distracted or give in to the urge to vent or complain. However, great teams rally quickly, center on optimism and use the right amount of analysis to craft lasting solutions.

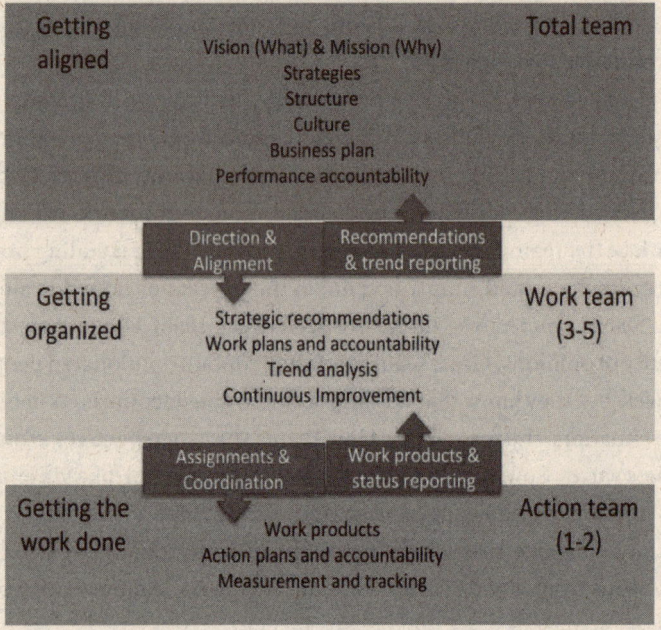

Figure 7

THE PROCESSES

Though they may not do so perfectly, all functioning teams do these four team processes:

1. Set up the team: Why do we exist? Who are we?
2. Plan the work: Align around how work will get done
3. Do the work: Execute the plan
4. Resolve issues: Navigate the problems, opportunities or other topics that arise

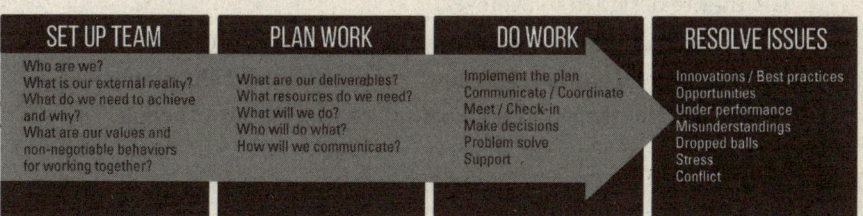

Some teams do these processes thoroughly, with great diligence. Other teams complete a cursory setup process, then get down to doing with little planning. Inevitably, this does not lead to team greatness.

Lest you think that this model is a linear one, remember this: All teams, great and not-so-great, cycle backwards. In fact, going back to review a plan after beginning the do stage is not seen as a negative. We'll address this more thoroughly in Chapter 5 and beyond.

> In the mid-1960s, psychologist Bruce Tuckman developed the model that many leaders have used to describe teamwork.[10]
>
> Forming: Team members want to be accepted and avoid conflict, and get busy organizing who will do what
> Storming: As issues arise, team members share differing opinions and conflict occurs, which may resolve quickly or linger for long periods.

---

10 Tuckman, B.W. "Developmental sequence in small groups." *Psychological Bulletin*, 63 (6) (1965): 384-399.

> Norming: The team agrees on a goal and makes agreements that will help them function toward that goal
>
> Performing: The team gets things done
>
> This model describes the processes teams go through as they get to know each other and begin working together, though some teams don't get too far past the storming phase. Those teams fail to overcome initial conflicts, don't develop positive relationships, and accomplish little, if anything, they're designed to achieve.
>
> Tuckman's model can help a team diagnose some basics, like "we're storming right now," but does little to help people navigate the dynamic reality of working with a group of people.

SET UP THE TEAM

Regardless of the team's purpose, every group of people needs to figure out the context in which they are working together. So, before they get down to doing stuff, they need to align and understand the internal and external reality. Stated simply, "What is the situation, and why do we exist as a team?"

When starting a new team, doing the required setup may seem like a no-brainer. Yet how many fledgling teams do a really thorough job of addressing these questions? Some teams give the setup step short shrift. Instead, they quickly move to planning activity, missing the opportunity to establish a solid foundation that will make every subsequent step more efficient and likely to be successful.

Doing setup well is a Green Path choice. It is choosing to CARE for the greater good with a high degree of COMMITMENT. Great teams stop to ask themselves these foundational setup questions, even if it means a short pause if they've already begun to function as a team:

- What is our reality? What outside factors must be considered? What issues are there within and outside of our industry? What context does the team operate in within the organization?
- Who are we? What is our team identity? What is our

leadership structure? What talent, culture, experience, ideology or language diversity exists? What are each team member's strengths and natural talents? What competencies do we have and which do we lack?
- What do we need to achieve and why? What is our charge and why is it important? What is the future we are trying to create?
- What beliefs and values underpin our work? What are our non-negotiable behaviors for working together? What behaviors must we exhibit? What behaviors will not be tolerated? What is important to us in our work together? How does the work of this team align with our personal, individual values?

Caution! Do not assume that a long-standing team has covered these topics well, or that all team members would answer them similarly. If you are joining an existing team, ask these questions of several team members to see if they answer them the same or at least similarly. If not, the team needs to revisit setup.

Long-standing teams can experience setup drift, as members join and leave the group or external factors impact this important foundation. The passage of time can lull even great teams into assuming they all still understand their purpose and goals in the same way. All teams—even great ones—must be vigilant to ensure that mutual understanding of these bedrock principles is maintained. An annual review of the key aspects of the team's setup can reduce or eliminate a gradual shift away from key shared values and identity.

PLAN THE WORK

You've joined a new team, and everyone is excited to charge forward. There can be an almost overwhelming urge to get busy and make things happen. Great teams resist the urge to start "doing" right away. First, they create a solid plan for how the work will get done. Preparation makes the difference between frantic activity (often in multiple directions) and strategic execution toward a specific, mutually-understood outcome. Key planning questions include:

- What are our deliverables? What interdependent results do we need to achieve? What is the desired impact?
- What resources do we need? Do we have the right people, money, time, experience and skills?
- What will we do? What are our key projects? What functions must happen? What are the processes that will ensure success?
- Who will do what? How will we divide the work, making the most of each team member's strengths? What are the clear accountabilities and responsibilities for each team member?
- How will we work together? How and when will we routinely communicate? How will communication protocols change when there are problems? How will we make decisions? What are our timelines? How will we adjust when our time estimates are off? What will we do when we disagree? When will we work solo, and what situations will maximize the return on collaboration? How will we sustain momentum and positive attitudes when the going gets tough? How will we conduct meetings and difficult conversations?

Great teams are not daunted by the many questions that the plan phase presents. They realize that stepping back to look ahead will set them up for success when they do get busy working the plan.

DO THE WORK

Time to get down to it. The groundwork has been laid for success. The team is aligned on what to do and the broad strokes of how to do it. The details are fleshed out and documented, and coordinated action can start.

Great teams are smart about every aspect of getting work accomplished. They understand how decisions are best made and problems are effectively resolved. They unleash creativity that would not be possible if each person were working solo. They coordinate their actions to achieve both efficiency and great results. They create the right communication channels and check in with each other frequently enough to stay aligned and accomplish their individual and collective goals. They support, challenge and encourage each other in achieving the outcomes that matter. In the end, they find the sweet spot of collaboration (see Chapter 4) that delivers results.

Key aspects of the "do" process are:

- Implementation plan. Create a more detailed, tactical plan for getting the work done, including key milestones and key performance indicators (KPIs) that will gauge progress.
- Action steps. Follow through on the plan, adjusting in small ways as necessary.
- Communicate. Get the right people involved at the right time, with the right level of detail. Share information freely, but make sure that communication is geared to what people really need to know. Otherwise, people can be inundated with huge amounts of information. That simply creates noise. Vital information, like values and vision, will need to be repeated, however, to ensure that everyone understands and is in alignment.
- Meet/check-in. This involves remote and in-person meetings that utilize agreed-upon meeting best practices. These meetings are driven by clearly defined outputs (what will be achieved). For example, rather than a topic like "discuss ABC production issues," an output-driven agenda item would be "agree upon strategies to decrease waste on lines A and C."
- Make decisions. There are many ways that teams generate options and make decisions. Some teams may prefer seeking complete consensus around decisions, and others prefer to move forward even if there is not 100 percent agreement. Regardless of the method of coming to the decision, what really matters to great teams is the degree of commitment

to supporting the solution. People can be less than 100 percent in agreement and still 100 percent committed to supporting it. Though people will buy in if they agree 100 percent, many durable decisions can also be achieved at 70 percent agreement. ("I can support this even if it isn't exactly what I want.")

- Get feedback. Seek input from within the team and from outside stakeholders so adjustments can be made to create better outcomes. All team members must be willing to discuss not only how the team's goals are progressing, but their own contributions as well. An open mind to feedback is necessary for individual and team greatness.
- Problem solve. Eliminate assumptions and define the problem and its root cause(s). Using team capabilities, brainstorm potential solutions. Remember that the team doesn't have to agree 100 percent, but they do have to be 100 percent committed to supporting the solution. Implement fixes that are effective for the current issue and prevent the problem from recurring. Rather than focusing on blame, learn from problems and come out of tough times even stronger.
- Support. Employ open, caring communication to support fellow team members, giving input and feedback routinely. Raise issues early and directly with the person(s) involved. Offer support without rescuing people, empowering people to be productive and accountable. Connect with fellow team members as people, not cogs in the machine.

EXAMPLE: SET UP, PLAN AND DO

A super simple example of these first three steps of team process involves planning an event. Sue and Anika work together to plan the elementary school science fair.

SET UP the Team: First, Sue and Anika decide on their focus

(science fair for three hours on an evening in March) and resources (the budget, committee, school staff, etc.) at their disposal.

PLAN the Work: Sue and Anika agree on the deliverables (student involvement, recognition/prizes and publicity), committee structure, meeting cadence and budget.

DO the Work: Sue and Anika contact committee members and hold meetings. At the meetings, Anika typically takes the lead, ensuring that all of their work is focused on the deliverables they need (transformative choices). Outside of meetings, team members take action to move the science fair plan forward.

ISSUES

All teams, great and not-so-great, must grapple with issues. Some of these will be pleasant surprises that present new opportunities for success. Others will be less pleasant challenges to overcome.

Take our science fair committee. One of the committee members completes only some of her assignments between meetings and tries to convince others (including the school principal) to make the fair competitive, with recognition only for the top three entries (an example of a manipulative choice). Also, several school staff communicate scheduling conflicts with proposed March dates for the science fair.

Issues occur whether your team is large, formal and complex or small, volunteer and relatively straightforward.

In spite of great effort and planning, all teams encounter situations that are unexpected and often unpleasant. Those may include communication issues, misaligned focus, changes in the external reality, etc. An absence of identified problems does not mean that the team is functioning at peak performance. And an abundance of problems is not an indication of a bad team. It's how the team handles issues that determines greatness, not the number of issues that occur.

The next chapter will examine the ways in which teams contend with the inevitable issues that arise.

CHAPTER 5: NAVIGATING ISSUES

THINK OF A TIME when you worked with a group of people toward a common goal, and something unexpected and unwanted occurred. How did the team react? Was the presence of an issue cause for alarm, or just a natural byproduct of working together toward a common goal? Was it "all hands on deck" to resolve the problem? Or did people look around for someone to blame? Was the team paralyzed by the situation and its potential risk?

Navigating issues is an essential aspect of teamwork, and yet so many of our experiences would lead us to believe two things:

1. Problems are bad and a sign that something is wrong.
2. Groups of people can't resolve issues very well.

Neither of these statements is true. At least, they are not inevitably true. The whole notion that teams should either be issue-free or a hot mess represents a duality that simply is in error.

It is vital to dispel the myth that great teams don't encounter issues as they work together. In fact, complications and unanticipated obstacles are just a part of life, and should be viewed as a routine part of work. (That is, they are routine unless they are a result of poor planning, lack of coordination or subpar performance. Those are preventable and should be viewed as such.)

In fact, when we work together with others, unexpected complications are common and normal. They happen simply because we cannot control everything about human flaws, the work itself and the environment in which we operate. External factors, like the economy or the weather, can impact the team's ability to succeed no matter how great they are.

Sometimes people simply make mistakes. Other times, team members are influenced by others' choices to engage in behaviors that are not helpful or positive.

Working with others is not easy and requires intelligent action, investment in the right things and consistent effort. If left to chance, teams will migrate inevitably to a Red Path.

> *"It is easy to hate and it is difficult to love. This is how the whole scheme of things works. All good things are difficult to achieve; and bad things are very easy to get."*
> —Confucius

Every single team runs into difficulties. People can work together to remedy problems and come out stronger in the end. Or they can give up, join the ranks of the uninvested and ensure that the team is not successful in reaching its goals.

What makes the difference between teams who implode when faced with obstacles and problems and the groups that rise to the occasion and tackle challenges head-on?

Choices.

The choice to respectfully confront a team member who is missing the mark.

The choice to bring a new idea to the table, even when it may not be popular with everyone.

The choice to stay late at the end of the day to accomplish something important.

The choice to change comfortable habits.

The choice to accept feedback that is difficult to hear and then do something about it.

These are examples of what we call Green Path choices. Green Path choices are ones that combine a focus on what's best for everyone (CARE), a high COMMITMENT to results that is sustained in spite of difficulties, self-awareness, and an ability to engage productively with others (PEOPLE intelligence). These qualities are especially needed when the going gets tough. And they can be in short supply when teams encounter roadblocks, unanticipated puzzles and other developments that can be stressful.

Green Path choices enable teams to confront and resolve thorny developments. They do what some leadership experts (though originally attributed to Woody Allen) advise; they show up. Even in situations where it would be easier to back off or ignore what's happening, they actively prioritize and use these behaviors:

- Caring, honest and direct communication
- Listen to understand
- Engage, align, learn and coordinate
- Share perspectives (including an emphasis on data-driven v. opinion)
- Focus forward on solutions

Like all teams, great teams face both opportunities and problems. Great teams don't always function perfectly. When misunderstandings, glitches or other issues arise, they are seen as a normal part of life and an opportunity to learn and grow. Rather than avoiding obstacles, controversy or stress, great teams dig in and engage immediately and actively.

Great teams avoid blame in times of trouble, instead focusing on problem resolution and achieving a higher level of performance. They work through conflicts as soon as they arise, with a focus on listening to understand each other's perspective.

Great teams recognize that unity isn't always for the best. Spirited and respectful debate is seen as a norm, and team members work hard to productively disagree and work together to find the right solutions.

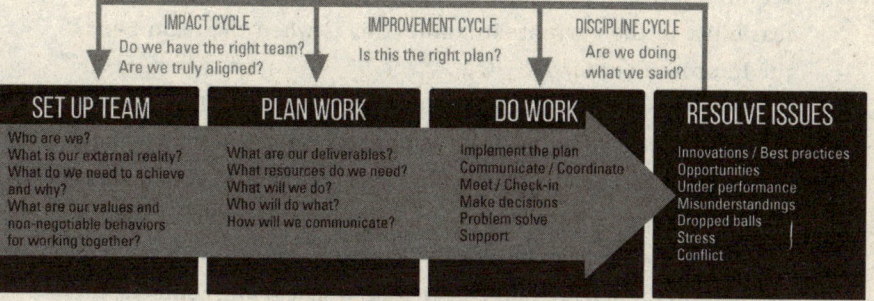

DISCIPLINE CYCLE

Let's go back to our science fair committee. One of their members decides to pursue her own agenda for the event, hoping to make it competitive and only recognize the top three ranked entries. The group also faces pushback on their scheduled date.

At the committee's request, Sue holds a one-on-one meeting with the rogue team member, attempting to refocus her on the goals of the fair (*productive* choice). She chooses to show respect and care for the other person's perspective. She directly communicates the direction of the group. Ultimately, the committee member resigns and her duties are spread among other committee members.

This is an example of the Discipline Cycle, when teams need to figure out if they're following through on what they agreed to do. The science fair committee reaffirmed their decision made in the setup process that they would keep the science fair as noncompetitive as possible in order to encourage more children to participate. The team member could not agree to this fundamental principle, and her resignation allowed the team to continue moving forward and focusing on their goals.

IMPROVEMENT CYCLE

The team is confronting problems, and they've ascertained that the plan is being implemented as designed. Some issues require more stepping back to examine the original plan and its feasibility in the current situation. This is when the team needs the Improvement Cycle.

The key question in the Improvement Cycle is "Do we have the plan right?" Sometimes, in spite of a team's best efforts, new information or changing conditions require them to do a course correction on the original plan. They may need to revise it slightly or give the plan a major overhaul.

Back to the science fair. Due to March scheduling conflicts, the planning team decides to hold the science fair in February. All of the timelines for deliverables are adjusted, and committee members get to work communicating the decision and getting their plans done. Due to a tighter timeframe, a couple of activities are deleted, but for the most part, the plan continues with a new timeline.

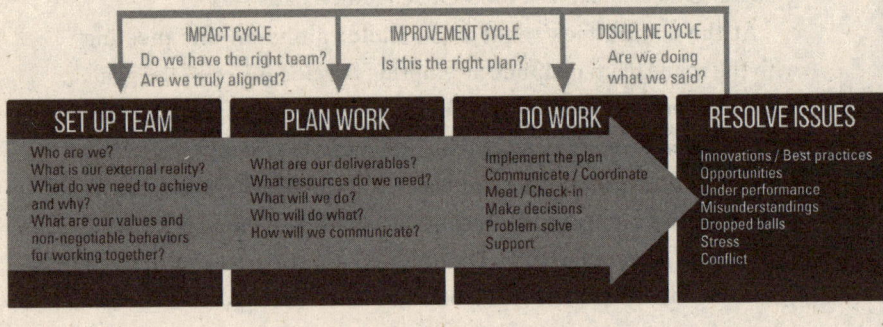

IMPACT CYCLE

Sometimes ensuring that everyone is implementing the team's plan—and that the plan is the right one—still doesn't resolve an issue. The team may need to go all the way back to reviewing their setup to make some adjustments.

Take our science fair committee, for example. After navigating some initial issues well, the committee realizes that they might have a lack of resources on the team. They meet to realign around the goals and deliverables for the event, and realize that it would be helpful to have at least one science teacher join the group. They brainstorm some options and get a volunteer to recruit a teacher as a team member.

Change is a constant. And it is one of the most common reasons for the Impact Cycle and the need to review and adjust the team's setup. Teams must adapt to ever-shifting environments within and outside of their organizations. This doesn't mean swapping out the boat every time the wind changes, but great teams make course corrections along the way to create a winning scenario.

GOING THROUGH THE CYCLES

When teams engage well, they move forward with clear expectations for all team members, and a renewed commitment to each other and the team's goals. There is increased trust. The team's journey through issues results in relationships that are stronger and individuals who are more resilient. Team members value learning and continuously improve so that they remain on course and achieve both tactical and strategic goals.

What did the science fair team accomplish after working the WGTDG process? An amazing science fair. Though there were issues along the way and during the evening of the event, it was considered a great success.

CONTAGIOUS CHOICES

One person's choices are often contagious, especially if that person is a team leader or is able to influence other team members. This can create a virtuous Green Path or destructive Red Path cycle on the team. A pattern of Red Path choices keeps the team on the Red Path.

While their collective choices do create momentum, teams don't have to get stuck. Each moment offers opportunities to make a Green Path choice, then an opportunity to make the next positive choice, the next and so on.

Human teams, rather than superhuman ones, are a patchwork quilt (or brick path) of green and red choices. Think of your current team. Is the path you're following paved with mostly green or red bricks? That will largely determine your current trajectory. And that trajectory can shift, as we will explore in the next chapter.

CHAPTER 6: MAKING YOUR TEAM GREAT (RED PATH TO GREEN PATH)

THE GREEN PATH IS transformative and is the source of team greatness. The Red Path, on the other hand, leads to team dysfunction and an inability to reach their potential. Red Path choices can result in open conflict and spectacular failure. Other times, the problems inherent in a team on the Red Path aren't so obvious.

To have a hope of developing into a great team, it's important to acknowledge where the team is operating today. Sometimes that can mean facing the ugly truth that many times the team chooses what's easy or comfortable, chooses self over the greater good and doesn't navigate emotions well. When it comes to teamwork, avoiding and accommodating Red Path choices can be silent killers. So now is the time to speak up.

Not sure where your team stands in terms of its path? Here are some behaviors of Green and Red Paths—visible (and sometimes subtle) symptoms that are a result of the team's pattern of choices.

WHAT GREAT TEAMS DO GREAT

GREEN PATH
- Caring, honest, and direct
- Listen to understand
- Engage, align, learn, and coordinate
- Share perspectives (data driven)
- Focus forward on solutions

RED PATH
- Dishonest, uncaring, or indirect
- Attack / avoid / freeze
- Ignore
- Accommodate
- Blame others
- Be defensive

SET UP TEAM
- Who are we?
- What is our external reality?
- What do we need to achieve and why?
- What are our values and non-negotiable behaviors for working together?

PLAN WORK
- What are our deliverables?
- What resources do we need?
- What will we do?
- Who will do what?
- How will we communicate?

DO WORK
- Implement the plan
- Communicate / Coordinate
- Meet / Check-in
- Make decisions
- Problem solve
- Support

RESOLVE ISSUES
- Innovations / Best practices
- Opportunities
- Under performance
- Misunderstandings
- Dropped balls
- Stress
- Conflict

IMPACT CYCLE — Do we have the right team? Are we truly aligned?

IMPROVEMENT CYCLE — Is this the right plan?

DISCIPLINE CYCLE — Are we doing what we said?

FAILURE CYCLE

DECLINE CYCLE

ATTACK / AVOID CYCLE

HUMANERGY

© copyright Humanergy

CHAPTER 6: MAKING YOUR TEAM GREAT

Green Path	Red Path
Accept that all success is interdependent	Care for self only
Commitment to impact	Commitment to comfort or safety or ease
Engage with people in a caring, honest and direct way	Treat people in an uncaring, dishonest or indirect way
Work to create emotional and physical safety	Be thoughtless or aggressive
Be authentic, vulnerable and show humility to learn	Be defensive
Listen to understand	Listen with an agenda, judgment or bias
Share perspectives	Shut down or lash out
Focus forward on positive impact	Blame others or continually bring up the past
Keep perspective on the critical few priorities	Be distracted by the trivial or too many priorities
Build win-win solutions together	Dominate and compete
Match resources to work	Engage in wishful thinking and be unrealistic in planning
Do what it takes for success	Don't try or give up when there are challenges

MOVE FROM THE RED TO THE GREEN PATH

You think your team is on the Red Path? How do you recover and get back to mostly making choices that reflect CARE for the greater good, COMMITMENT to impact and high PEOPLE intelligence?

1. Recognize the Red Path. This is a two-part process. First, are YOU on a Red Path? Before you start pointing a finger at your

teammates, examine your own choices. Own your own "stuff" before you analyze the behavior of others. At a team level, a single miscommunication or disagreement doesn't mean the team is on a bad trajectory. Your team is on the Red Path if they exhibit consistent or reoccurring patterns of behavior that are:

   a. Self-oriented

   b. Geared toward comfort

   c. Reflecting an inability to navigate internal or interpersonal emotions

See the right column above for the Red Path symptoms. Occasional Red Path choices do not necessarily derail a team. However, if one or more of these symptoms is common, recurring and creating discord or poor performance, it's time to go to step two.

2. Engage. Gather the team and have a caring, honest and direct conversation.

   a. Review the qualities of transformative choices:

      i. CARE for the greater good, which includes everyone, the organization, etc.

      ii. COMMITMENT to impact. People may not always be comfortable, and making a difference can sometimes mean stretching oneself, learning and growing.

      iii. PEOPLE intelligence. Team members manage their own emotions well, expressing them when necessary in a constructive manner. They engage with each other in sensitive and unreserved ways and navigate collaboration and conflict well.

   b. Discuss the team's reaction to Red Path choices. Common responses are similar to the reactions to trauma—fight or flight. Some team members may engage harshly and others may check out. Without placing blame on anyone, consider the spillover effects of these fight and flight reactions.

   c. Review the cycles, in order (Discipline, Improvement and

CHAPTER 6: MAKING YOUR TEAM GREAT

Impact), until the root cause is determined.
    i. Discipline: Are we doing what we said we would do?
    ii. Improvement: Is the plan right?
    iii. Impact: Do we have the right resources and are we truly aligned?

The next chapter focuses on true stories (fictionalized to protect client confidentiality) of teams on the journey to greatness.

CHAPTER 7: WHAT GREAT TEAMS DO GREAT IN ACTION

All organization names have been changed, as have some of the details, to protect the privacy of our clients. In some cases, the examples used are composites of teams we've worked with. Any resemblance to an actual company or team is purely coincidental.

VAE INDUSTRIES

VAE INDUSTRIES HAD BEEN operating its plant in Sutterville since the 1970s. VAE Industries' twelve plants manufactured a variety of automotive components. The company tracked key metrics (like waste, safety, unit production, etc.), and Sutterville was at the bottom for every single one.

Joe Sambiano, the new plant manager, knew he had a challenge on his hands. His observations of the site's top leadership didn't make him feel more confident. This group of thirty operated in cliques and silos, rarely approaching any situation with unity or sustained commitment. Though all of the leaders were frustrated about Sutterville's inability to improve, they engaged in practices that ensured failure. They pitted their own departments against others, held grudges against their peers and rarely accepted responsibility for their own mistakes.

When it came to managing their direct reports, VAE Sutterville's leaders were heavy-handed and punitive. As the situation worsened, they intensified their efforts, calling workers out publicly and regularly threatening people's jobs. They seemed to emulate the leadership attributed to Captain Bligh of the stricken HMS *Bounty*, against whom the mutineers revolted in 1789. While flogging sailors for small infractions of the rules, he is said to have declared, "The beatings will continue until morale improves."

SET UP. This wasn't Joe's first plant turnaround project. He knew that he needed to break the cycle and create a new VAE Sutterville. He scheduled monthly one-day off-site work sessions with senior leaders. Joe clarified expectations for results (what they had to achieve), the stakes involved and the new normal for how they were going to operate as a team. Some of the nonnegotiables for working together included open communication, zero tolerance for backbiting, and a culture of mutual respect and encouragement.

Did the plant's leadership embrace this new approach? Generally, no, at least at first. Initially, there was much resistance and cynicism. Joe kept moving forward, and got the team of leaders involved.

PLAN. At these leadership off-sites, Joe and the team identified the high-priority areas or "leverage lines," parts of the plant where there was the greatest revenue potential and thus the biggest potential impact. Together, they created a plan to focus resources and attention on maximizing the efficiency and effectiveness of these lines. Joe focused first on getting alignment among peers. Silos were broken as leaders were forced to work across departments. They quickly realized that they needed to build the capacity of frontline leaders, so they worked together to develop a supervisor leadership training series for shift supervisors and team leaders.

DO THE WORK. Within months, VAE Sutterville began to

see a measurable impact of the changes due to the focus on high-potential lines and their new ways of working together. There was still some resistance to the changes instituted by Joe. Over time, however, as the team directly addressed problems and stopped sweeping interpersonal issues under the rug, the resistance waned. Success was recognized and people were applauded for their efforts. Joe's leadership team was amazed that time in meetings was actually being reduced. That's because report-outs were focused on what was necessary for moving forward, rather than long reviews of the extraneous details or rants about what was going wrong. Sutterville still had its challenges, and the hours were long and sometimes frustrating. But overall, work was more satisfying and rewarding.

ISSUES. The VAE Sutterville off-sites were key to creating an open and engaged environment where issues were addressed directly. This proved more challenging for some leadership team members than others. A few leaders weren't able to get on board with the new way of engaging with each other. They were reassigned to less impactful and influential roles. Others, reluctantly, were laterally assigned to address an urgent need. Though it wasn't their choice at the time, in most cases these people later appreciated the reasons for the move and the value of the assignment for themselves and VAE Sutterville.

GREEN PATH. Transforming daily choices didn't happen overnight. Joe, the plant manager, worked with his coach to get feedback about how to transform the "Red Path" culture into one that was more transformative (high CARE for the greater good, high COMMITMENT and high PEOPLE engagement). Like most culture transformations, this started with the top leaders modeling a new way of engaging. Joe, working with his coach, set the example for vulnerability, open communication and engaging the team in tough conversations. Before too long, the needle started to move as more of the Sutterville leadership began to choose "Green Path" behaviors.

DISCIPLINE CYCLE. No more sweeping problems under the rug at VAE Sutterville. Thanks to choosing open team communication and transparency, issues and challenges were regularly identified and addressed both in off-sites and weekly team meetings. The "blame game" gave way to a choice to review problems as learning opportunities. Over time, this discipline would cascade down to departments, who started to operate in the same way.

IMPROVEMENT CYCLE. Some of the issues identified required going back to the drawing board and admitting that plans and tactics weren't paying off the way the team had hoped. Beginning with Joe and a couple of key leaders, there was a real focus on using data to amend any plan or procedure that wasn't getting the necessary results. Sutterville's leaders let go of previous choices (e.g., defending a process because it was familiar or Person X's idea, ignoring a failing tactic or ignoring the facts and going with the gut). They were willing to dig deep to understand what was going on and then create a new strategy that would get them better results.

IMPACT CYCLE. Joe was excited. The plant's numbers didn't lie. It became apparent throughout VAE Industries that Sutterville was changing. After one year, they were no longer bottom on all the metrics, and after two years, they were top on all but one (where they were second). They were reaping the benefits of having the right people in place, doing the right things. Corporate even authorized some minor capital improvements that improved efficiency. The leadership team realigned regularly, due to turnover. This was due to a few team members being tapped for promotions and transfers throughout the enterprise. Clearly, VAE Industries wanted to spread the transformation that happened at Sutterville.

THE REST OF THE STORY. The Sutterville plant was seen as a success story throughout VAE Industries. Some corporate people wanted to replicate the success but wanted to shortcut the process. They weren't willing to invest in the off-site time and the daunting task of truly aligning the leadership team. Not surprisingly, these half-hearted attempts failed. Sadly, though Sutterville thrived, the entire industry suffered; ultimately all of the plants were either shut down or sold to a holding company. Many of the Sutterville leadership team went on to senior roles in other organizations, replicating the success in these new facilities using similar processes.

A funny sidenote. Pre-WGTDG, two Sutterville leaders spent years being adversaries, keeping their departments strongly siloed and regularly feeding their mutual antipathy. Two years after starting this team transformation process, these two were close associates and even took their families on vacation together.

What Great Teams Do Great transforms people in unexpected ways.

BLUFFTOWN FOODS CUSTOMER SERVICE

BluffTown Foods (BTF), a consumer packaged goods (CPG) corporation, had a long history of market domination in snacks and frozen foods. BFT was also widely recognized as a role model in creating and maintaining a positive corporate culture, evidenced by a value for teamwork and camaraderie that was even described as "the BFT family."

The customer service group (CSG) of BluffTown Foods had a track record of successfully representing BFT with customers, while being the "face" of the customer for the company as well. They recognized that customers' experiences were defined by the integrity, skill and quality of the support received from the customer service group. In addition, the CSG played a vital role in providing insight to the company about customers' preferences, perspectives and needs.

BFT as an organization was in the midst of transformation. Changes in people's eating habits, a volatile commodities market, an expansion of smaller brands, the explosion of digital engagement and virtual retail options all combined to create disruption in this century-old, global organization. These market factors resulted in the larger BFT organization going through a leadership, strategic and cultural shift.

Long-held values which had been the "true north" for BFT's people now seemed to be cast aside, though they were still technically espoused as "the BFT Way." Integrity, respect and open communication were largely replaced with a competitive, win/lose and siloed culture. The company's direction seemed unpredictable, so teams hunkered down and tried to survive or clashed (passive aggressively or even openly), hoping to retain power and autonomy.

The stated culture of BFT was no longer the real culture. This fact showed itself in the annual employee experience surveys, which indicated a decline in morale, climate, trust, teamwork and engagement.

The customer service group was a good team, even when the organization around them was struggling. They had always been focused and had a strong commitment to making a positive impact on the company's trajectory. CSG team members at all levels believed in and lived "the Green Path." As a result, their team always scored well on employee engagement and culture surveys.

However, they saw the "perfect storm" of eroding profits, unclear strategy and toxic culture coming. Their evolving reality meant that being good wasn't going to be good enough. The CSG needed to be a great team in order to thrive, or even survive. They needed more resilience and better performance to exist in a corrosive and even destructive corporate environment.

So the CSG made a bold move. They decided to become an island of sanity in the midst of chaos and a beacon of quality for others to emulate. And even if others did not follow their lead, CSG team members would commit themselves unconditionally to creating a great team that did the right things for the company for the right reasons.

SET UP. The CSG had a long history of mostly operating in the "Green Path," but they were operating in a sea of "Red Path" choices. The old best practices for working together, derived from the code of conduct for BluffTown Foods, were no longer adequate. They needed a new set of foundations that formed a documented, cascaded and embedded set of practices to guide what they did and how. These behaviors were necessary for their sustained success in the midst of turmoil and combativeness.

The CSG leadership used their annual retreat as a work session to define a new recipe for success. The recipe included practices like transparency, taking ownership for solutions, listening to understand, gaining alignment and buy-in from key stakeholders and building trust. This recipe was what would keep the CSG team both sane and productive in the midst of chaos and dysfunction.

PLAN. The "recipe for success" was a set of practices that could only be accomplished with a focused, consistent effort. The CSG team developed an active schedule for rolling out, reinforcing and embedding the recipe into daily operations. This plan included a set of rescue strategies that would be employed if the team felt it was straying from these key best practices or not meeting their targeted metrics.

DO. The recipe for success became part of all team discussions and performance reviews. Posters, brochures, videos and other communications provided constant reinforcement of the behaviors that kept them doing the right thing for the company and their people. Rather than being an "extra," the recipe was integrated into every team member's role and activities.

ISSUES. No team, even a great one, can avoid issues. The CSG team operated within a very challenging environment—both within the company and due to a constantly-evolving customer base. Key stakeholders did not always operate in ways that were consistent with this recipe. And CSG team members didn't operate within the recipe 100 percent of the time. As problems occurred, they were analyzed not only from the lens of tangible work products and processes; the recipe also provided a means for evaluating the "how" of their work as well. When people strayed from those practices within the team, they received immediate feedback, in a respectful and caring way, to refocus on the choices that built and sustained their success. Monthly reviews of the recipe for success, a six-month formal reassessment, and as-needed, situation-specific analyses kept the team on track.

GREEN PATH. Over time, CSG team members developed a safe harbor for themselves, making daily choices that aligned with their values, as articulated in the recipe for success. The CSG team was seen as a beacon of sanity in an otherwise unsettled environment.

DISCIPLINE CYCLE. The CSG team openly dealt with issues as they arose. Sometimes those were positive, like new opportunities to build customer partnerships and transform relationships. Other issues were less fun, but they had a positive lasting impact. Recognizing that conflict and disagreement were good for the team, they did not hesitate to raise contentious issues. Their recipe for success helped them be successful in this regard, as they focused on listening, getting alignment and moving forward productively.

IMPROVEMENT CYCLE. The CSG team used the improvement cycle to adjust and adapt the plan for the recipe integration on a monthly basis. Some responsibilities were shifted and plans amended to keep this vital recipe both front of mind and acted upon daily.

IMPACT CYCLE. Throughout the course of the first year, several team members were reassigned to other duties due to company cutbacks. This necessitated a review of the team's setup, including a rethinking of resources, given the cuts. The team worked together to ensure that their key functions continued to run smoothly, and that the recipe for success remained a central part of the team's functioning.

THE REST OF THE STORY. BFT routinely conducted annual workplace surveys. CSG was the workplace star standout for three years, even as the surrounding departments continued in their downward spiral. As BFT continued to downsize, most displaced CSG staff were either retained or were shifted to new jobs, often with an increase in influence and responsibility. Staying on the Green Path paid off, even as the larger organization continued to struggle.

GREENFIELD UNIVERSITY MBA PROGRAM

Greenfield University's weekend MBA program brings together over 100 leaders who work full-time as they complete their master's in business administration degree. They are organized by Greenfield

University MBA staff into study teams, and 40 to 50 percent of the individual's grade is dependent on the team's performance.

Executive MBA students learn about leading and influencing teams through a course facilitated by David Wheatley and other Humanergy staff throughout their entire EMBA experience. The objectives are to know how to build and lead effective teams, grow as team members, use that study team experience to recognize high performance, and to be able to influence peers and hold team members accountable.

Learning about teams begins immediately. On the first day of the program's weekend orientation, they each meet around five strangers who will make up this team that can make or break the experience and outcomes. Humanergy works with them at the beginning of the program and bi-monthly during the first year to ensure they learn about what makes great teams great and put that knowledge into practice.

How well (and quickly) their team comes together to develop and implement exemplary practice determines not only each team member's grades; it can also mean the difference between a difficult experience (like all intensive EMBA programs) and one that is chaotic and even brutal.

SET UP. During their first weekend together, Humanergy facilitates a process that helps team members get to know each other a little and align around what they all see as success. This starts with each team member's list of goals/achievements, like a 3.9 GPA or work/life balance. The teams are guided to take these personal visions of success and create one for the team. At the orientation, they explore the underlying values and behaviors necessary for working together effectively.

PLAN. The orientation concludes with the group confirming an initial plan/outline for how they will work together, who will do what, how decisions will be made, best practices for communication and how problems will be solved.

DO. The work starts at the intensive week, when all students are in residence at Greenfield and give their undivided attention to three classes. This involves full days of class combined with a great deal of late-night work, both as a team and individually. There are many required work products and lots of pressure to get them done, individually and together.

Informal and formal opportunities are presented to the students in order to evaluate the quality of their do-ing. This includes a formal assessment about five months into the program. Each executive MBA team evaluates the degree to which they are still aligned on their shared goals and agreed-upon best practices.

ISSUES. The intensive week, with its tight timeframes and multiple deliverables, inevitably results in issues like miscommunication or conflicting goals. Other teams seem to start strong but find that in the first months of the program they lapse in their alignment on goals or use of best practices.

Study teams face an important crossroads. Do they forge ahead and try to ignore the problems that arise? Or do they, as a group, address them productively and create solutions? Even if the issues aren't serious at this early juncture, do they dive in and use these opportunities to grow individually and as a team? To do so means a better chance of success that endures.

Up-front planning at the orientation puts many teams at an advantage when it comes to the inevitable challenges. They know how they'll process issues, and that makes adapting their earlier plan easier.

GREEN PATH. At the five-month point, study teams reevaluate their success card (what they want to achieve and how they will do it). They complete a survey to gauge the extent to which their team (and themselves) are aligned on their success definition (goals) and using the best practices they identified during the orientation. Through this process, study teams identify the types of the choices they are making individually and together. Some study teams recognize that they are already starting to take the Red Path. They are avoiding issues, engaging in unproductive conflict, or looking for who to blame when things go off the rails.

Other teams find this reevaluation confirms and reinforces what they are doing well—their Green-Path choices. Study teams that get the best results and enjoyment from the program are on the Green Path. For that reason, study teams embarking on a Red Path are provided with additional facilitation services to help them move forward productively.

DISCIPLINE CYCLE. The Discipline Cycle asks the simple question, "Are we doing what we said we would do?" Greenfield's study teams receive their survey results and begin to understand whether they're really doing what they said they would do during orientation. In other words, are they still aligned to the set of goals they identified a few months ago? Secondly, are they using the best practices they committed to during their first weekend together? If not, why? Was it a lack of real alignment or enduring commitment? Was it simply drift or competing commitments? Some study teams need to revisit their success definition or best practices and either recommit or refine them. Others find that they are doing the agreed-upon processes to reach their goals but are still not achieving the results they want. Those teams need to move on to the Improvement Cycle.

IMPROVEMENT CYCLE. Study teams may need to rework the plan. Perhaps they decided that weekly chat-room communication would be the way they kept on target for deadlines. At the time, that seemed like a good idea. However, based on some missed targets, they now know that aspect of the plan isn't working for them. They may choose to have a weekly face-to-face videochat instead of relying on the chat room. Regardless of the specifics, the Improvement Cycle ensures that all aspects of the plan are tweaked so that they work well; these adjustments ensure that there is agreement and commitment to the key deliverables, each person's key roles and responsibilities, and ways work moves forward.

IMPACT CYCLE. A few teams find that they are implementing the plan as described and feel the plan is solid, and yet problems persist. They aren't getting the results they want and need. Those teams need to go back to the basics of setup and realign on any of these foundational questions about working together.

Some teams wrestle with the fact that they were naive about the reality of doing an EMBA program and navigating hectic lives. Others realize that they had not been completely transparent about the values they brought into the study team. Regardless of the specific reasons, these teams need to regroup as it relates to the basics of team structure, purpose and goals.

Some may jump to the conclusion that having to go all the way back to setup means that the team is not great, maybe even not good. On the contrary, it can be a sign of real team greatness that they are willing to go back through all aspects of the cycles to get alignment and commitment to moving forward.

THE REST OF THE STORY. Study teams, when operating on the Green Path, find the process enriches their experience of the MBA program, both in terms of tangible results, like grades, and the less tangible aspect of reduced stress. Many team members become lifelong friends, supporting one another through professional as well as personal circumstances long after their eighteen-month MBA program concludes.

CHAPTER 8: ISSUES AND ANSWERS

THE FOLLOWING ARE EXAMPLES of typical team scenarios and how they apply to the What Great Teams Do Great model. They are presented in terms of an issue overview and suggested actions to get on the path to team greatness.

Issue 1: People on the team are frustrated. They feel like they're going in circles and working on disparate goals. There is little sense of common purpose, so people do what they think is best on any given day.

Action:
- It is easy to become siloed, with people focused on their particular role or even working in opposition to one another. To get and keep alignment (and reduce the frustration that misalignment can cause), do not assume that everyone is on the same page. Even teams that start out with a clear picture of success and good best practices can drift. Every team needs to stop and check themselves at regular intervals to ensure that they are focused on common goals and agree about how to get there.
- Stephen Covey used to talk about hacking through the jungle

and every so often climbing a tree to make sure you were in the right forest. If we don't pause to look at the big picture, we can do a lot of work with zero sum gained. That's what happens when we are working against each other or creating redundancy. See https://leadershipforlife.wordpress.com/self-managing-leadership/leadership-and-management-by-stephen-r-covey/
- Work the cycles. It's probably necessary to go back to at least the plan for the work. Realign to the plan, and perhaps even go back to review the team's setup if the issue remains. Alignment has a shelf life, so regular check-in/alignment sessions keep people focused on the what, why and how of the work.

Issue 2: Everyone is busy putting out daily fires. Priorities shift a lot, based on immediate needs. Team members don't feel like they have the time to address teamwork, mutual goals or greatness.

Action:
- Work back through the cycles. Begin with the Discipline Cycle. Are we doing what we have said we will do? If not, then why? If so, the plan needs review. Is it a thorough plan? Is it the right plan to achieve what you need as a team? If not, use the Improvement Cycle to amend the plan.
- Take the Green Path; engage people in alignment conversations around where this work fits with other priorities. Be honest with each other as to capacity and priority. Ensure that listening to understand is a value, and show respect while being 100 percent up front about the situation.
- If this seems like a lot of work, remember the old saying that we "never have time to do it right, but we always make time to do it over." Mediocrity will never be overcome without stopping and figuring out how to do the right things the right ways as a team.

- Busyness can be a death spiral that drives Red Path behavior—see the VAE example in Chapter 7. Constant firefighting is a sign that the team needs to stop and find the root causes. Even real firefighters recognize that 90 percent of fighting fires is prevention, not racing around from one emergency to the next.

Issue 3: Team meetings stink! How are we going to build a great team if we can't focus, have productive conversations, reach team consensus and act on our decisions?

Action:
- Team meetings should be work—the right, good work that is necessary for success. It may be that some things that are being dealt with in meetings should be done in other ways, like individual work followed by review. There are really only four reasons to meet: 1. Make a decision; 2. Ensure understanding and alignment; 3. Engage creativity; 4. Team development.
- A team meeting is just a mini-version of the cycles; meetings require a clear output (setup) and plan (agenda) and should always be driving progress toward the larger goals.
- Make Green Path choices in meetings.
  - Caring, honest and direct communication
  - Listen to understand
  - Engage, align, learn and coordinate
  - Share perspectives (including an emphasis on data-driven v. opinion)
  - Focus forward on solutions

Issue 4: The team struggles to communicate. Some people seem unwilling or unable to share much information with others, often citing busyness as a reason for not communicating. Meetings don't seem to help much, as many participants are quiet for all or most meetings.

Action:
- "What we have here is a failure to communicate," said the captain in the movie *Cool Hand Luke*.
- There are many reasons for a lack of communication, in meetings and otherwise. People may feel so busy that they want to remain quiet, keep their heads down and get on with what they feel they need to do. Team members may be fearful and protect information as a means to achieve job security. This may not be a rational response, because poor performance results from a lack of appropriate information sharing. And poor performance may well get someone fired before being the "keeper of all knowledge" becomes useful.
- The most common reason for a lack of communication is that it's hard to get right. Communication is challenging—because people aren't good at it or the systems for achieving and keeping clarity haven't been established. Don't assume that people know how to communicate well. Train people in both listening well and communicating clearly. Most importantly, create a space where people feel safer speaking up. Open communication as a norm should be emphasized in setup and every aspect of how the team operates.
- In meetings, group size or power dynamic may be intimidating. Therefore, find time to break into smaller groups with good questions to stimulate engagement by everyone. Most people will be happier sharing in this smaller setting, and as the larger groups hear the report-out, valuable input will be gained.

Issue 5: The team hates conflict. Members want to "get along," yet there is an undercurrent of tension that is unresolved. Some people avoid certain individuals on the team, rather than deal with the issues. Others employ passive-aggressive tactics.

Action:
- Avoiding conflict just delays the inevitable confrontation and makes it worse. Accepting this as reality means that the best time to address the issue is now or as soon as reasonably possible. The commitment to address any significant issue within twenty-four hours (if at all possible) should be a part of the team's charter at the time of setup. If it is not, then it's time to review and realign on the setup for the team.
- Where a team fears conflict, use the WGTDG model to create the conversation. The tool itself provides a language and framework for people to address issues without the fear of things getting too personal.

Issue 6: The team is in conflict. Some team members make personal attacks or aggressive plays for control. Others duck for cover, hoping to stay out of the fray.

Action:
- First, all team members need to make sure they stay on the Green Path and don't get sucked into the red behaviors. This applies to those directly involved and those that are on the periphery.
- Review the reasons the team is a team, and what the team is trying to achieve together. This is part of setup.
- Engage the team in identifying clear expectations of how they should work together. Engage them to get buy-in and commit to the expectations they agreed to at setup.
- Assume positive intent. It may take some engagement with the warring parties, but it is important to recognize that no one is trying to be difficult. Assume that people are doing their best, or at least have a positive intention, or the negativity will multiply.
- Help everyone place a value on listening to understand.
- Create a plan for moving forward more productively.

CHAPTER 8: ISSUES AND ANSWERS

Issue 7: The team leader doesn't like to make decisions or hold people accountable. Team members have high individual standards but want to have more leadership to address common goals. There is frustration about the leader's inability to remove barriers to success.

Action:
- The regular review of the Discipline Cycle provides the opportunity to identify the issues around team leadership.
- Speaking with the team leader about the lack of leadership requires deep transformative choices. There must be a strong commitment to the greater good, a willingness to focus on impact, and the people skills to frame up the team's needs while challenging the leader to step up into his or her role.
- With this mindset, a person or small group from the team should sit with the team leader to explain the concerns and offer assistance to get back on track.
- Listen to their perspective and understand what is causing the issue.
- Focus on what the team needs to achieve and necessary timelines.
- Be supportive without being directive.

Issue 8: The team lacks energy and imagination. The group is unable to generate fresh ideas and perspectives and doesn't turn unexpected events into opportunities. Instead, they go back to established patterns of behavior.

Action:
- They have fallen into the death spiral of Red Path passive choices.
- To break the norm, the group needs to revisit the setup box to remind themselves why what they are doing is important.
- Realign and potentially change things up (team personnel). Break the normal by taking the team off-site or to a different location.

- Engage in team-building events that drive creative thinking, and then focus on how they can apply the same learning to work.
- Ask different questions than you have been asking. If you are getting the same answers, you are probably asking the same questions.

Issue 9: A newly-formed team is struggling to quickly get up to speed. Some team members barely know each other's names, let alone how their roles intersect.

Action:
- Invest a significant chunk of time in helping the team get to know each other (i.e., at least a half-day, if not a couple of days with an evening activity between them).
- Use tools such as Myers-Briggs or DiSC to help the team understand who they have and what they bring to the table.
- Map roles with the group: What do they think is their role? What do they think is others' roles? Using post-its, capture and re-sort to aid clarity.

Issue 10: One team member with low morale is bringing everyone down. A long-term employee, it seems unlikely that this person will be fired or relocated.

Action:
- In a respectful and caring way, hold this individual accountable for the expected behavior; don't back off just because they have tenure.
- Give direct feedback (including specific behavioral examples) and support them in identifying the issues that contribute to the morale issue.
- Coach the person to create baby steps of change to move in the right direction.

- Document your actions and if necessary look for off-ramps to more suitable roles.

Issue 11: The team isn't bought into the goals that the organization wants them to adopt. Several team members have voiced concerns about whether the goals are realistic.
Action:
- Engage the team in an open conversation about the organization's targets.
- Be realistic and transparent. Don't try to sugarcoat the situation, and be honest about what is real/fact and what is supposition/opinion.
- Think CIMA. Realign the team to focus on where they have control and influence; there may be aspects of this process that they have to mitigate (reduce negative impact). Everything else must be accepted as a reality that cannot be changed.

Issue 12: The team has a "superstar" who takes credit for everyone's work, constantly elevates himself and is driving others nuts with his constant self-promotion.
Action:
- Have direct, honest and caring conversations one-on-one with the individual about this behavior; give specific examples of what has been observed.
- Engage to help the person understand why the behavior is happening.
- Engage team in mini-360 session. Give feedback on specific behaviors and what the person should stop, start and keep doing to improve.

Issue 13: The team is risk-averse. Due to some backlash over past mistakes, team members play it safe, duck and cover and don't reach their full potential.

Action:
- Charting a course to a future reality can be exhilarating. It also requires a tolerance for risk, since the journey to your ultimate destination will include some surprises. Mark Twain said to succeed in life you need two things—ignorance and confidence. The team may not know exactly what lies ahead, but start the "trip" by figuring out what it is the team really wants to achieve. This will activate excitement and hopefully courage to overcome risk aversion.
- Start with smaller, easier-to-achieve goals. Rather than biting off a big, risky venture, set more achievable goals that won't push the risk threshold too much. Slowly amp up with harder-to-achieve and riskier plans (with high reward).
- Don't become cavalier about risk. Be aware of the potential problems inherent in every move, and don't let that stop the team from taking calculated action that carries with it some degree of peril. However, there must be a calibration between risk and potential reward. That will require a strong vision, alignment and open communication.

APPENDICES
MISSING COMPONENTS OF WGTDG

Components	What if it is missing or handled badly?
Set up	**Headless** The team lacks focus and leadership. There is no clarity or alignment. Confusion exists as to who is on the team and what the team mission is. There is a lack of buy-in, and team members don't energetically "show up."
Plan	**Footless** There is little or no clarity or alignment as to what to do and who should do what. This obscurity results in dropped balls and misunderstandings. Team members experience lots of treading water and spinning wheels.
Do the work	**Paralyzed** There is little or no follow-through on the plan. Work is not aligned to the plan or not much happens at all. People slowly lose interest and focus on other things.
Issues	**Blind Red Path** Not addressing issues doesn't mean they go away. If left unaddressed, the team will fall into Red Path behaviors. Results will suffer or be nonexistent.
Discipline cycle	**Attack/avoid cycle** When results are not what they should be, the team has an important choice to make. Do they address it by asking the first question, "Are we doing what we said we would do (the plan)?" Unfortunately some teams don't want to face what's going on. They avoid this discipline cycle and either put their heads in the sand and ignore the problems, or they try to figure out who is to blame.

Improvement cycle	Decline cycle It can be very frustrating to have to go back to the team's plan and make changes. However, that is what must happen if the results are not what they need to be and the plan has been implemented as designed. Avoiding the improvement cycle results in decline, as the team continues to spin its wheels doing the same things that were not getting the right results in the first place.
Impact cycle	Failure cycle The failure cycle happens when people avoid examining the team's setup. Instead of facing the fact that some of the roots of the team need attention, they continue to flounder until failure is inevitable. To avoid this cycle, use the impact cycle to explore every aspect of the team's foundation—its purpose, mission, composition, resources, etc. This can and should feel like a reboot of the team.

GLOSSARY

Accept: What you cannot impact; you have no impact on performance driver and no impact on performance results

Accountability: Evaluation and support necessary to create change in performance

Action Plan: Written goals with specific behavioral strategies created to create a change or new result in behavior, procedure, competence, etc.

Behavior: How one acts, functions or reacts

Best Practice: Documented step-by-step instructions and/or standards that should be consistently followed for tasks or projects to avoid errors and subpar results

Calibrate: To adjust precisely for a particular function; people must calibrate to the realities of any situation in order to understand what they can control, influence and mitigate. All other aspects must be accepted

Care: An object of concern or attention. In the context of leadership, is there concern for the greater good (including the self) or the self alone?

Choice: An act of selecting or making a decision when faced with two or more possibilities

Choice Space: Time dedicated to choosing behavior, rather than acting out of habit or impulse

Choices of Leadership: A Humanergy model used to plot the types of leadership behaviors based on the degree of commitment to the choice, focus of concern (self v. others) and people intelligence

CIMA: A calibration tool used to determine which factors one can control, influence, mitigate and accept in a situation; used to focus time and energy

Close the Loop: After careful listening, summarize a person's statement in one's own words to ensure clarity and mutual understanding.

Collaborate: Work with others to achieve something

Commitment: The state or quality of being dedicated to a cause, activity. In the context of leadership, this is the degree to which one is dedicated to success, in spite of difficulties or roadblocks.

Competence/competency: Desired thinking, behavior and results which are habitual and fluid

Control: What you can do; 100 percent impact on performance driver and 100 percent impact on performance results

Cue: What triggers a habitual behavior; for example, waking up can be a trigger for making coffee.

Cycle: A series of behaviors which occur (with or without intention) that move a team in a positive or negative direction

Delegation: The transfer in ownership of a task or responsibility

GLOSSARY

Discipline: Activity or experience that provides mental or physical training; regularly monitoring and measuring individual and team performance results and impact, making adjustments as necessary

Discipline Cycle: Process of assessing whether the team has been doing what they said they would do (implementing the plan)

Emotional Intelligence: The ability to monitor one's own and others' emotions and to use this information to guide thinking and acting. Also referred to as people intelligence.

Emotion: Neurological reactions to a stimulus

Engage: To establish a meaningful contact or connection with; the opposite of engagement is remaining aloof, uninvolved or passive.

Failure Cycle: The point at which teams either regroup on their fundamentals (setup) or face complete failure. This is the end stage of a team's evolution if it continues operating on the Red Path.

Feeling: The conscious experience of emotions or the meaning you assign to the brain's emotions

Green Path: A proactive response to conflict that leads to a high performance cycle

Habit: A settled or regular tendency or practice, especially one that is hard to give up

Habit Loop: A neurological loop that governs any habit. The habit loop consists of three elements: a cue, a routine, and a reward. Together these elements of habits reinforce the behavior.

Impact: The effects of the outcomes (results) achieved; for example, effective communication and alignment results in production goals being met, and the impact is organizational profitability.

Impact Cycle: Part of the Green Path, this cycle involves reevaluating and refocusing on the fundamentals of the team, including team membership, alignment on purpose and goals, etc.

Improvement Cycle: Part of the Green Path, this cycle occurs when a team understands that it has been implementing the original plan as intended and still is not achieving the right results or impact. Reevaluation and replanning are necessary to create a new plan for team success.

Key Performance Indicators (KPIs): Specific, measurable elements to measure progress toward a specific outcome; used for accountability in delegation

Kotter Model: An eight-step model used to successfully create organizational change (Source: Kotter, J. "Why Transformation Efforts Fail" HBR Mar-Apr 1995)

Leader: A person who makes a choice to invest in the greater good of the group

Mutual Understanding: A shared picture and alignment that is the result of successful communication

Path: The combination of the types of choices made by a person or team

People Intelligence: The ability to monitor one's own and others' emotions and to use this information to guide thinking and acting. Also referred to as emotional intelligence.

Plan: To decide on or arrange in advance; in the context of teamwork, groups of people engage with one another to map out their intended goals, best ways of working together and assignments for team members.

Red Path: A reactive response to conflict that leads to a low team performance cycle (Source: What Great Teams Do Great model)

Results: The outcomes achieved through behavior, processes, etc.

Reward: The reinforcing benefit one gets from engaging in the routine response (e.g., smell, taste and energy boost of coffee made after waking up)

Routine: The automatic behaviors associated with a cue (e.g. preparing and drinking coffee upon awakening)

Self-awareness: Accurate understanding of your thinking, behavior and results

Setup: The fundamentals of the team, including composition, external factors, key purposes, values and guidelines for behavior, etc.

Slippery Slope: The idea that raising conflictual ideas is easier if done earlier and directly, rather than avoiding difficult topics, which creates a larger and more intractable set of problems

Stop, Think, Choose: Technique for gaining emotional composure before reacting. Stop—make a choice space. Think—what is important, and the degree to which there is mutual understanding. Choose—follow through with actions.

Sweet Spot: An optimum point or combination of factors or qualities that produce the best results (for example, the sweet spot of collaboration involves the right people and the right number of people using optimal processes)

Team: Any group of people who want or need to get something done together

Thinking: Self-talk (internal dialogue), one's understanding, beliefs and values

Track: Simple monitoring of performance progress

Transformative Discussions: A process for productively addressing issues or topics that are potentially conflictual or highly emotional in an open, honest and caring manner

Trust: Firm belief in the reliability, truth, ability, or strength of someone or something

What Great Teams Do Great: A Humanergy model for team best practices that achieve amazing results

ACKNOWLEDGMENTS

All great projects involve more than the direct team, with tangible effort, amazing support and care for the process, people and final product. First we would like to thank the other Humanergists who have worked with and contributed to these tools over the last 20 years: Lance Satterthwaite, Corey Fernandez, Jim Marshall, Michelle Kunde and Will Ellis. Our wonderful operations team, Karen Weideman, Tiffany Funk, Pat Vanhorn and Uhdav Doctor, inspired clear thinking, focus and action.

We would also like to thank some key clients who have supported the development of these tools by their implementation, including, Cheri Declerq and Greg Janicki and the many students of MSU's EMBA; the wonderful Brazeway team; as well as Dan DiSebastian, Larry Reid, Gianni D'Angela, Scott McFarland, Bob Boisture, Chris Sargent and many others who continue to take the green path in their everyday leadership.

Last but not least, to our families, some now scattered to the four winds and citizens of the world... Launda, Josh, Joe, Tevy, Polinia, Shannon, Ryan and Maggie.